Four Pillars of Constitutionalism

R

CONTAINS THE FULL TEXT OF:

THE DECLARATION OF INDEPENDENCE

THE ARTICLES OF CONFEDERATION

THE NORTHWEST ORDINANCE

THE CONSTITUTION

Four Pillars of Constitutionalism
THE ORGANIC LAWS
OF THE UNITED STATES

Introduced by
Richard H. Cox

 **Prometheus Books**

59 John Glenn Drive
Amherst, New York 14228-2197

Published 1998 by Prometheus Books

02 01 00 99 98   5 4 3 2 1

Library of Congress Cataloging-in-Publication Data

Four pillars of constitutionalism : the organic laws of the United States / introduced by
    Richard H. Cox.
        p.   cm.
    Includes bibliographical references.
    ISBN 1–57392–215–3 (alk. paper)
    1. Constitutional history—United States—Sources. 2. Constitutions—United
States. I. Cox, Richard Howard, 1925–   .
KF4502.F685   1998
342.73′029—dc21   98–18635
                                                                  CIP

Printed in Canada on acid-free paper

CONTENTS

PREFACE AND ACKNOWLEDGMENTS   7

INTRODUCTION   9

Lincoln and Brennan on the Constitution   11

The Location and Character of the Organic Laws   14

The Constitution as Organic Law or as Constitutional Law?   17

The Organic Laws in the Nineteenth Century
  A. Legislative History of the Official Versions
     of the Laws of the United States   26
  B. The Terminology of "Organic Laws"
     in the American Experience   36

C. Political Reasoning on the
    Nature of the Organic Laws   41
    I. Lincoln's Statesmanship
        1. The Speech on the *Dred Scott* Decision   42
        2. The Cooper Institute Speech   49
        3. The First Inaugural   53
    II. Congressional Debates in the Nineteenth Century,
        and Especially the Era of Reconstruction,
        1865–1875   57
        1. The Declaration of Independence   58
        2. The Articles of Confederation   61
        3. The Northwest Ordinance of 1787   63

Constitutional Restoration   66

Continuous Founding   71

THE ORGANIC LAWS OF THE
UNITED STATES OF AMERICA   73

The Declaration of Independence (1776)   75

Articles of Confederation (1777)   84

Ordinance of 1787: The Northwest Territorial Government   97

Constitution of the United States of America (1787)   106

SUGGESTED READING   139

PREFACE AND ACKNOWLEDGMENTS

I have two purposes in presenting this book to the public: First, I seek to make readily available to my fellow citizens, in a reasonably priced volume, the authoritative text of the documents which constitute the four pillars of American Constitutionalism: the Declaration of Independence, the Articles of Confederation, the Northwest Ordinance of 1787, and the Constitution of the United States. Second, I seek to gain a hearing for an argument for making a return to the nineteenth-century understanding of the Constitution as "*the* organic law" of the American Republic, indeed, as the culmination of the three antecedent "organic laws." That argument, set forth in the Introduction, serves as a prologue to the text of the four documents. Its point of view is that of a citizen writing for his fellow citizens.

I owe the idea for the book to Harry V. Jaffa. I learned from him some years ago—to my profound and somewhat embarrassed surprise—that at the very beginning of the *United States Code* stands a section titled "The Organic Laws of the United States." Surprise

7

gave way to curiosity, curiosity to inquiry, and inquiry at length to the Introduction of this book.

Peter Baxter, as a graduate student, helped with the initial research. Paul Cornish then did truly yeoman service in seeking out old laws and new volumes, pursuing leads and running down facts.

Robert Faulkner and Paul Dowling read the draft of the Introduction. Their questions, comments, suggestions, and, above all, their intelligent criticisms, made that part of the book much better than it otherwise would have been. The faults that remain I can claim for my own.

Steven L. Mitchell, Editor-in-Chief, and Paul Kurtz, President, of Prometheus Books, saw fit to take on this project. I am grateful to them for their willingness thus to contribute to civic enlightenment.

INTRODUCTION

I am naturally anti-slavery. If slavery is not wrong, nothing is wrong. . . . And yet I have never understood that the Presidency conferred on me an unrestricted right to act officially upon this judgment. . . . It was in the oath I took that I would, to the best of my ability, preserve, protect, and defend the Constitution. . . . I understood . . . that in ordinary civil administration this oath even forbade me to practically indulge my primary abstract judgment on the moral question of slavery. . . . I aver that, to this day I have done no official act in mere deference to my abstract judgment on the moral question of slavery. I did understand, however, that my oath to preserve the Constitution to the best of my ability, imposed upon me the duty of preserving, by every indispensable means, that government—that nation—of which that constitution was *the organic law.*

President Abraham Lincoln (April 1864)[1]

---

1. "To Albert G. Hodges," in *The Collected Works of Abraham Lincoln,* Roy P. Basler, ed. (New Brunswick, N.J.: Rutgers University Press, 1953), VII:286. (Emphasis added)

[T]he Constitution is a sublime oration on the dignity of man. . . .
It is a vision that has guided us as a people . . . although the precise rules by which we have protected fundamental human dignity
have been transformed over time in response to both transforma-
tions of social conditions and evolution of our concept of human
dignity. . . . The Framers discerned fundamental principles
through particular malefactions of the [English] Crown. . . . But
our acceptance of the fundamental principles has not and should
not bind us to those precise, at times anachronistic contours.

Justices of the Supreme Court are not Platonic guardians
appointed to wield authority according to their personal moral
predilections. . . . We look to the history of the time of the
framing and to the intervening history of interpretation. But the
ultimate question must be, what do the words of the text mean in
our time. For the genius of the Constitution rests not in any static
meaning it might have had in a world that is dead and gone, but
the adaptability of its great principles with current problems and
needs. What the constitutional fundamentals meant to the
wisdom of other times cannot be their measure to the vision of
our time. . . . Those who would restrict claims of right to the
values of 1789 specifically articulated in the Constitution turn a
blind eye to all social progress and eschew adaptation of over-
arching principles to changes in social circumstances. . . . [But]
the demands of human dignity will never cease to evolve. [And]
the unique interpretive role of the Supreme Court with respect to
the Constitution demands some flexibility with the respect to the
call of *stare decisis* [judicial precedent]. Because we are the last
word on the meaning of the Constitution, our views must be subject to revision over time, or the Constitution falls captive . . . to
the anachronistic views of long-gone generations.

Supreme Court Justice William J. Brennan (May 1985)[2]

---

2. The full text of Justice Brennan's speech is contained in a collection titled
"Addresses: Construing the Constitution," in *University of California (Davis)
Law Review* 19, no. 1 (Fall 1985): 2–14. I have, of course, selected only small
portions of the speech for the epigraph, but I believe they capture the gist of
Brennan's understanding.

These statements sketch two distinguished Americans' understandings of the Constitution as a whole and the duty owed to it by one who holds high public office and who, accordingly, has sworn to uphold it.[3] We, as citizens, naturally must wonder which understanding is more persuasive, or even whether they are ultimately reconcilable. Let us therefore begin by focussing on key aspects of each statement.

LINCOLN AND BRENNAN ON THE CONSTITUTION

Lincoln calls the Constitution "the organic law." What precisely he means by that phrase, and why he chooses it, are unclear, for it is terminology that is today very unfamiliar. But reflection on the whole of his statement indicates that for Lincoln the Constitution, as "organic law," forms and gives direction to the government and the nation; that it lays upon him, as president, an oath-based responsibility to "preserve, protect and defend" it; and that it forbids him from using the powers of his office, out of adherence to his own abstract moral judgment, peremptorily to bring an end to the greatest evil ever to afflict the American Republic, that of the enslavement of Negroes.

Turning momentarily from Lincoln's statement to the text of the Constitution, we find that his phrase "preserve, protect and defend" is an exact excerpt from the oath he took when becoming president. In reflecting on this fidelity to the text of the Constitution, we may also next observe that Lincoln thrice emphasizes the duty to "preserve"—the government, the nation, and the Constitution. He thus seems to single out "preserving" as the first duty, and to construe

---

3. The specific oath required of the president is in Art. II, Sect. 1, Para. 8. Art. VI, Para. 3 states that "judicial officers . . . shall be bound by oath or affirmation to support this Constitution," but does not specify the oath or affirmation.

"protecting" and "defending" as means to that end. We may then again wonder what exactly he means by characterizing the Constitution as "the organic law" which he is oath-bound, above all, to "preserve," and what exactly he understands to be the proper means for "protecting" and "defending" it. A preliminary suggestion is that Lincoln means by "the organic law" the Constitution of the Framers; that he understands their instrument to be due that "sacred reverence, which ought to be maintained in the breasts of the rulers towards the constitution of a country," as had been stated by Publius, in 1787, in *The Federalist*; and that one means by which both to "protect" and "defend" it is to speak reverently about it with the utmost precision, thoughtfulness, and eloquence.

Brennan never speaks of the Constitution as "the organic law." His highest praise for it is as a "sublime oration on human dignity." He at times pays respect to the Framers of the Constitution, to their "wisdom," and to "principles" they embodied in the Constitution, although at times he also appears to equate "principles" with "values" or "ideals." He imputes to the Framers a commitment to a basic concept of "human dignity" in framing the Constitution. But he suggests that their understanding of that concept has proven, in the light of subsequent history, to have been "static" and applicable only to a "world that is dead and gone." Indeed, Brennan perceives the concept of human dignity to have been in constant "evolution," from the time of the Framers' founding to 1985, and to be inexorably and desirably evolving further into the wholly indefinite future.

Accordingly, though he insists that it is the duty of the justices of the Supreme Court to eschew resort to "personal moral predilections" in deciding cases before the Court, Brennan also conceives that it is their duty to give great—perhaps absolutely decisive—weight to the evolving understanding of human dignity in so deciding. What is more, he holds that it is the Supreme Court which has a "unique interpretive role" with respect to the Constitution, for it is that body which has "the last word on the meaning of the Constitution." Given these two premises, this conclusion ineluctably follows: the content of human dignity guaranteed by the Constitution must undergo constant reformulation by the justices of the Supreme Court and their understanding of it is final and controlling. In short, Brennan's understanding of the Constitution and of the role of the justices echoes a famous pronouncement of Charles Evan Hughes: "We are under a Constitution, but the Constitution is what the judges say it is."[4]

I am well aware that this brief contrast of Lincoln's and Brennan's understandings is not conclusive as to which is the more persuasive, let alone as to whether they are ultimately reconcilable. Indeed, the contrast as I have sketched it barely outlines the nature of the tension between the two modes. But it is sufficient as an entry point into the underlying issue of how we, as citizens, should understand the Constitution, beset as we are with conflicting claims on that vital point. In what follows, I give the bare bones of an argument and present some detailed evidence to justify my own conclusion: that we as citizens should make a deliberate return to understanding the Constitution as the ultimate organic law of the American Republic and that Abraham Lincoln is our surest guide for making such a return.

To reach that conclusion, I begin with a sketch of the location and character of "the organic laws" in the federal laws of the United States. I then also quickly contrast the Constitution perceived as organic law to the Constitution perceived through the refracting lens of a certain understanding of constitutional law, which is the dominant mode within present-day American political science and law. I next turn to a somewhat detailed historical treatment. Here I focus on the nineteenth century, in three related modes. First is a

---

4. Samuel Hendel, *Charles Evans Hughes and the Supreme Court* (New York: King's Crown Press, Columbia University), p. 11. Hughes made the statement in 1907, when governor of New York. He amplified the statement in 1908: "The Constitution, with its guarantees of liberty and its grants of federal power, is finally what the Supreme Court determines it to mean." Ibid., p. 12. Hughes was Chief Justice of the Supreme Court from 1930 to 1941.

sketch of the legislative history of the enshrinement of the organic laws as the preamble to the statute laws of the nation. Second is an inquiry into the terminology of organic law. Third, and most crucial, is an analysis of the political arguments which lend support, in the nineteenth century, to the understanding of the Constitution as organic law. The key arguments here are those set forth in three speeches by Lincoln. I next turn to a brief reprise of the contrast of Lincoln's and Brennan's understandings of the Constitution, and some suggestions for further reading. These are intended to lend support to a project of constitutional restoration, a project which would again place the organic laws, as organic laws, at the center of the study of the Constitution. I end with a proposal that we as citizens may engage in a "continuous founding" in thought.

THE LOCATION AND CHARACTER OF THE ORGANIC LAWS

Anyone who has access to the latest edition of *The United States Code* (1994), the federal government's official publication of the "General and Permanent Laws of the United States," will readily discover that the very first section of *The Code* is titled "The Organic Laws of the United States of America." He will also readily discover that this section contains four fundamental documents: (1) *The Declaration of Independence—1776.* It is the organic law which states the principles of natural right, denominated as self-evident truths, justifying the thirteen states' uniting for the revolutionary overthrow of the rule of England. (2) *The Articles of Confederation—1777.* It is the organic law which first binds the newly independent states together and which states the principles of government of what is repeatedly called a "perpetual union." (3) *Ordinance of 1787: The Northwest Territorial Government.* It is the organic law which states the principles of government for the vast territory in what we now call the upper Midwest, principles among which, most notably, is an explicit prohibition, rooted in the principles of the Declaration of Independence, against the introduction of slavery into all that area of the burgeoning republic. (4) *Constitution of the United States of America—1787.* It is the organic law which states the purposes of "We the People of the United States" and the frame of government which they have ordained and established in the Constitution.

The Organic Laws thus stand as a kind of noble preamble to the whole body of federal statute law, which now comprises fifty titles. However, anecdotal evidence I have accumulated over the past several years indicates that few present-day lawyers, judges, and professors of political science or law—those who are specialists in the treatment of government and law—are even aware of the existence of that first section of *The United States Code.* What that obliviousness may signify is a point I will take up momentarily in a brief discussion of typical present-day constitutional law textbooks.

There is no preface to the Organic Laws section; no explanation of how, when, or why it came to be the first section of *The United States Code.* There is no explanation of "the organic laws," a phrase that is puzzling because it is today so unfamiliar. On the other hand, as perusal of the four individual texts quickly shows, there are some terse, fairly detailed footnotes to portions of all the documents except the Ordinance of 1787. But there is no explanation of how or by whom those notes were appended to three of the documents. Thus the Organic Laws section, as we most immediately encounter it, proves to be a puzzling mixture of clarity and obscurity.

Bothered by the obscurity, I set out a few years ago to find answers to the how, when, why, and by whom questions. During the course of my inquiry, I became increasingly aware that the Organic Laws section is rooted in an understanding of the Constitution that is now largely in eclipse. It is my intention, in arranging for publication of a readily available edition of the four documents, and in preparing these introductory remarks, to bring that understanding out from behind the eclipsing body of the dominant mode of treatment of the Constitution within American political science and law.

In seeking the origin of the Organic Laws section, I discovered, after digging around in old dusty volumes, that it has existed for well over a century, for it first graces the porch of federal statute laws in 1878.[5] I will later present a more detailed historical analysis of the reasons for and the significance of that development. For now, it suffices to note the bare-bones details of how this came about: On March 2, 1877, Congress passed an act stipulating that the president should appoint a single commissioner to review, revise, and correct the newest official version of the laws of the United States; and that the commissioner should include "the Articles of Confederation, the Declaration of our National Independence, the Ordinance of seventeen hundred and eighty-seven for the government of the Northwestern Territory, the Constitution of the United States." President Rutherford B. Hayes appointed George S. Boutwell, then secretary of the treasury, as the commissioner. In September 1878, Boutwell signed the preface to the new official version of the laws. At the head of the statute laws he placed the title "The Organic Laws of the United States of America," and then the text of the four documents, in the order in which they stand in the 1994 edition of *The United States Code*.

---

5. I have drawn heavily on two publications for the history and character of federal legislation authorizing compilations and publications of the laws: J. Myron Jacobstein, Roy M. Mersky, and Donald J. Dunn, *Fundamentals of Legal Research*, 6th ed. (Westbury, N.Y.: The Foundation Press, 1994), pp. 163–67; and Erwin C. Surrency, "The Publication of Federal Laws: A Short History," *Law Library Journal* 79 (1987): 469–85.

THE CONSTITUTION AS ORGANIC LAW OR AS CONSTITUTIONAL LAW?

A generation after his action, as commissioner, in placing the Organic Laws section at the head of the official laws of the United States, Boutwell, as citizen, published a book titled *The Constitution of the United States at the End of the First Century* (1895).[6] Its structure is as follows: It begins with a section titled "The Organic Laws of the United States," and presents the texts of the documents exactly as they appear in the laws of the United States. It then gives the amendments to the Constitution, up to 1895, and an analytical index of the entire text of the Constitution. Boutwell's own contribution begins with three chapters of historical and interpretive analysis which are devoted to the first three organic laws and cover thirty-three pages. The four fundamental texts and these first three chapters, taken together, occupy nearly one hundred seventy pages of a four-hundred-page book. They serve as a remarkable preamble, as it were, to the actual discussion of the Constitution.

What is more, when Boutwell at long last turns to the Constitution, he at once enters upon an historical and interpretive analysis of the Preamble, then proceeds, article by article, to a similar inquiry into the whole. Along the way, although he presents brief summaries of important court decisions, he always does so within the perspective of the primacy of the fourth organic law, the Constitution, to which those decisions are subordinate.

The basic premises underlying both Boutwell's 1878 action as commissioner and as author of his 1895 book are these: First, careful study of all four of the Organic Laws is permanently relevant to, indeed essential for, a proper understanding of the Constitution. Second, the principles embedded in the Organic Laws are

---

6. Boutwell's book was republished, apparently as part of the celebration of the bicentennial of the Constitution, in 1987 (Littleton, Colo.: Fred B. Rothman & Co.).

ultimately those that go back to the Founders: the natural rights of man; the law of nature; and republican government, based on the consent of the governed, as the one true mode by which to give institutional effect to such rights and such law.

Boutwell's premises and his mode of treating the Constitution bear a striking resemblance to those found in a nineteenth-century American genre which, today, is largely unknown except as a matter of antiquarian inquiry—that of "commentaries" on the frame of government and the laws. Authors of the American commentaries took as their model a famous English prototype—Sir William Blackstone's *Commentaries on the Laws of England* (1765–69), a work of great authority among American colonists in the period prior to independence. The new commentaries were specifically focussed on the American frame of government and laws that came into being in 1789. Until early in the twentieth century, these commentaries were the dominant mode for teaching American citizens, neophyte lawyers, legislators, and judges about their constitutional system.

Two of the most notable American commentaries were those by James Kent and Joseph Story. Kent's *Commentaries on American Law,* first published in 1826–27, was about to enter a sixth edition at the time of his death in 1846, and achieved a remarkable fourteenth edition in 1896. Story's *Commentaries on the Constitution* was published in 1833 and was read, studied, and widely cited for the rest of the nineteenth century. It went through five editions, the last published in 1905, about a decade after the last edition of Kent's book.

Story was for many years both a professor of law at Harvard and an associate justice of the Supreme Court. Given this close connection between theory and practice regarding the fundamental law, it is particularly important to take note of the general approach and the structure of his once famous commentary, for it is a distinguished work in its own right, and also seems to have served as a model for writers such as George Boutwell. Story divides his three-volume treatise into three parts: "History of the Colonies," "History of the Revolution," and "Constitution of the United States." He begins the last part with a lengthy treatment of the general nature of the Constitution taken as a whole, including a discussion of the principal objections to the Constitution that emerged in the ratification debates, and a response to these. He then states nineteen rules of interpretation. Perhaps the most important of these is that the Constitution "is to be construed as a *frame* or *fundamental law* of government, established by the PEOPLE of the United States, according to their own free pleasure and sovereign will."[7] Story thus echoes the sense of purpose and the origin of the government that are articulated in the Preamble to the Constitution.

Only after this lengthy introduction does Story treat the text of the Constitution. He begins with the first words of the Preamble, "We the People of the United States, in Order to form a more perfect Union. . . ." His treatment of the fifty-two words of the Preamble, remarkably, occupies fifty pages of volume I. With this analysis and interpretation as a foundation, Story then makes his way methodically through every part of the Constitution, article by article. As he proceeds, both in treating the Preamble and the body of the Constitution, he calls attention to relevant historical material; he treats points contested in debates in the Federal Convention and in the ratification debates; he refers to arguments by other commentators; he adduces the reasoning of relevant court decisions; and he states his own view of a given provision. True to his own fundamental principle of interpretation, Story subordinates court decisions on key issues to analysis, historical observations, and reflection on the text. Story's magisterial way of treating the Constitution is rooted in the pervasive premise that the Constitution must be seen as an integral whole; that it is fundamental; and that its principles can be discerned, clearly stated, and defended.

In the century or so since Boutwell's book and the last editions

---

7. Joseph Story, *Commentaries on the Constitution of the United States* (New York: Da Capo Press, 1970), Vol. I, Section 409, p. 393. (Emphasis in original)

of Kent and Story were published, a remarkable change in the formal study of the Constitution has taken place. Today, the dominant mode of such study in both American law schools and American departments of political science is "constitutional law" as set forth in textbooks with that title. It is a study carried out by what is called the case method.[8] It focuses almost entirely on decisions handed down by federal courts and, most crucially, of course, by the Supreme Court. It typically posits the rightness of "judicial review" of legislation and executive actions as exercised by the Supreme Court. It often articulates the judgment that the Court is the one true and final arbiter in controversies concerning the meaning and application of the Constitution. It typically relies very heavily on writings by legal scholars. In short, over the past century, judges, legal scholars, and political scientists trained in the case method have become our principal teachers about the Constitution, and what they mostly teach is what people like themselves opine concerning our fundamental law.

How and why this very substantial change has come about during the last century is much too long and complicated a story for this Introduction to the Organic Laws. However, I have given some suggestions, in the later parts of this Introduction, in the notes, and in the bibliography for study of this topic. It is sufficient here to call attention to some of the main features and consequences of the last century's developments before turning to a much more detailed examination of how and why the Organic Laws came to occupy the preeminent place they do in the official text of the laws of the United States in the nineteenth century.

Consider, first, the status—or, to speak more accurately, the utter lack of status—of the Organic Laws within the present-day study of constitutional law. A survey of more than twenty texts of this kind, all published from the 1970s to the 1990s, reveals that all

---

8. For a trenchant critique of this development, see Gary McDowell, "Legal Education and the Constitution," *Benchmark* 1, no. 1 (January–February 1984): 14–18.

but one are simply oblivious of even the existence of the Organic Laws section of the federal laws of the United States, let alone its possible relevance to the study of the Constitution. The one possible exception I have located is a four-volume work titled *Treatise on Constitutional Law: Substance and Procedure.*[9] It is remarkable in that it does at least contain the texts of all four Organic Laws. But those texts are relegated to an appendix at the beginning of volume IV. What is more, there is no indication that they are the first section of *The United States Code*, or that they have the title "The Organic Laws of the United States." And given the huge bulk and high cost of this four-volume treatise, I seriously doubt that it is intended or used as a basic textbook of constitutional law. Thus, for all practical purposes, the existence of the Organic Laws section of the laws of the United States remains steeped in oblivion even in this weighty treatise.

Consider, second, the way in which the Constitution as such is treated in the most widely used modern-day constitutional law texts. Understandably, the text of the document is always included, often at the beginning. On occasion, there is also a brief historical prologue. But in contrast to the way taken by a Boutwell, a Kent, or a Story in the nineteenth century, there is in today's typical textbook no extended analysis and interpretation of the document taken as a whole. Whether this is because authors of such books consider that to be a superfluous activity on the premise that the general meaning of the Constitution is self-evident and easy to apprehend; or that such meaning is only to be found in court decisions and glosses by legal scholars; or worse still, that it has no fixed meaning at all, is unclear.

But it is worth turning for a moment to consider three features of the treatment of the Constitution in one widely used textbook of constitutional law, Harvard Professor Laurence H. Tribe's *American Constitutional Law* (1988).

---

9. Ronald D. Rotunda and John E. Nowak, *Treatise on Constitutional Law: Substance and Procedure,* 2d ed. (St. Paul, Minn.: West Publishing Co., 1992), 4 volumes. See vol. IV, pp. 684–806.

First, in stark contrast to Story's fifty-page treatment of the Preamble, as the proper prologue to analysis of the Constitution's articles, Tribe's textbook has no substantive treatment of the Preamble whatever, nor is the Preamble even mentioned in the extensive index.

Second, in contrast to Story's straightforward approach to the entire Constitution, Tribe's textbook is organized around what he calls "Seven Models of Constitutional Law": (1) separated and divided powers, (2) implied limitations on government, (3) settled expectations, (4) governmental regularity, (5) preferred rights, (6) equal protection, and (7) structural justice. None of these so-called models has a clear, direct basis in the text or structure of the Constitution. They are, in fact, abstractions developed by legal scholars, who now increasingly simply assume that such abstractions constitute an intrinsically more valid approach to the Constitution than does that of a Story.

Third, in contrast to Story's principle that the Constitution is the fundamental law, and that it is a coherent document with an ascertainable meaning rooted in permanent principles, Tribe proffers this "thesis" at the outset:

> . . . the Constitution is an historically discontinuous composition; it is the product, over time, of a series of not altogether coherent compromises; it mirrors no single vision or philosophy but reflects instead a set of sometimes reinforcing and sometimes conflicting ideals and notions.[10]

---

10. Laurence H. Tribe, *American Constitutional Law,* 2d ed. (Mineola, N.Y.: Foundation Press, Inc., 1988), p. 1. It is worth noting the first sentence of the course description of Constitutional Law in the 1997–1998 catalogue of Harvard Law School: "A study of basic principles of constitutional law as created, confused, compromised and changed by the Supreme Court." It is also worth noting the first sentence of an advanced seminar on Constitutional Law titled— ironically?—"Foundations of Constitutional Wisdom": "In the current post-Realist age, it is widely assumed that constitutional decision makers must make value choices in deciding constitutional questions."

Underlying and informing this remarkable shift in understanding regarding the very nature of the Constitution is an abstruse doctrine called "historicism." According to *Webster's Ninth Collegiate Dictionary* "historicism" apparently first came into American usage in 1914 and is a "theory that emphasizes the importance of history as a standard of value or as a determinant of events." As such, it is a doctrine simply unknown to the Founders or to commentators such as Story. It has its roots in European philosophical systems, most notably that of the great German philosopher, G. W. F. Hegel (1770–1831), whose *Lectures on the Philosophy of History* sets forth the fundamental thesis that all thought is essentially reflective of the spirit of the times in which a thinker happens to live. That thesis and corollaries thereof made their way into the study and teaching of American political science and law in the latter part of the nineteenth century, often introduced by American scholars who had gone to study for a time in Germany.

Nor is historicism the only philosophical doctrine to have had a profound effect on the study of constitutional law in the twentieth century. A terse formulation of the larger development, its consequences for understanding the Constitution, and a ready acceptance of those consequences is stated by Thomas C. Grey, who, when he wrote, was a professor of law at Stanford University. Grey states: "Intellectually, the 18th-century philosophical framework supporting the concept of immutable natural rights," which was embedded in the Declaration of Independence and in writings such as those by Story, "was eroded [since the latter part of the nineteenth century] with the growth of legal positivism, ethical relativism, pragmatism, and historicism." These abstract terms are, of course, utterly alien to the Constitution, and are unlikely to be known to the average citizen. But over time they have come to underlie and inform the treatment of the Constitution by many legal scholars.

That development has had enormous consequences. For Grey goes on to speak of the recent "development of constitutional rights" which are "clearly—and sometimes avowedly—not de-rived" from specific parts of the text of the Constitution, such as "the right to privacy." Grey concludes:

> The intellectual framework against which these rights developed is different from the natural-rights tradition of the founding fathers—its rhetorical reference points are the Anglo-American tradition and basic American ideals, rather than human nature, the social contract, or the rights of man. But it is the modern off-spring, in a direct and traceable line of legitimate descent, of the natural-rights tradition that is so deeply embedded in our consti-tutional origins.[11]

It is a large and difficult question as to the accuracy of Grey's claim that the present-day dominant intellectual framework for the interpretation of "rights" is one of "legitimate descent" from the "natural-rights tradition." But what is beyond question is that that tradition, so embedded in the Organic Laws, as we shall soon see, is today largely ignored or at best given lip service in much of the scholarship in present-day American political science and law.[12]

Reflecting on developments such as those I have just sketched, and more broadly, on developments within the dominant mode of treating American constitutionalism within American political sci-ence and law, Harvey Mansfield trenchantly characterizes our situ-ation as we near the end of the twentieth century:

> We speak constantly of rights and frequently invent new rights that a free of [*sic*] civilized people cannot do without. . . . But we

---

11. Thomas C. Grey, "Do We Have an Unwritten Constitution?" *Stanford Law Review* 27 (1974): 717.

12. An elective course at Harvard Law School, for 1997–1998, is titled "American Democracy." The course description says, in part: "The attempt throughout is to exemplify the work of a programmatic imagination that, informed by an understanding of social realities [earlier referred to as "the class, racial, and gender divisions of society"], frees itself from a *superstitious attach-ment to established institutions.*" (Emphasis added)

take for granted the Constitution that secures rights and forms the government. . . . We regard the Constitution as instrumental to the policies that are instruments to our rights. As our instrument, the Constitution is not above us; it is not to be honored, revered, looked up to. Accordingly, today it is not the object of scholarly study, either in political science or law. . . . Legal scholarship on constitutional history hardly exists today, and legal publicists use the Constitution to supply an aura for rights without really believing in its power, often while denying that power.[13]

This characterization of our situation surely can be and is contested. And as we shall see in the latter part of this Introduction, Mansfield's own writings on American constitutionalism may properly be said to be a contribution to modest-sized but worthy scholarly movement which Richard G. Stevens calls "Constitutional Restoration."[14] But as a characterization of the *dominant* mode of treatment of the Constitution within present-day American political science and law, it strikes me that Mansfield is squarely on target.

That said, it remains to consider what contribution a serious reestablishment of the Organic Laws, taken in their entirety, as the proper focus of a study of the Constitution, may make to clarifying where we should now seek to go. But to see the relevance of so doing, it is necessary to make a sustained effort to leave behind the present modes of thought and terminology and to return, for a time, to those of the nineteenth century in America. It is necessary, that is, to recover and think carefully about the meaning of a vocabulary and a way of looking at the Constitution which are today largely in eclipse. I point out the way to such a return by next considering the

---

13. Harvey C. Mansfield Jr., *America's Constitutional Soul* (Baltimore: The Johns Hopkins University Press, 1991), p. 184.

14. Richard G. Stevens, "The Prospects for Constitutional Law," *The Political Science Reviewer* 26 (1997): 273. The entire essay is a valuable review of developments referred to in the text, including reviews of some important books contributing to that restoration. A few of those books are referred to in the penultimate portion of this Introduction.

legislative, terminological and, most crucial, political history of the nineteenth-century treatment of the Organic Laws.

THE ORGANIC LAWS IN THE NINETEENTH CENTURY

A. Legislative History of the Official Versions of the Laws of the United States

On March 4, 1789, the Constitution of the United States superseded the Articles of Confederation. Henceforth, the lawmaking actions of the Congress and the president produced a new body of statute laws. From 1789 to 1795, the laws were simply published in newspapers, for no provision was made for their official publication. On March 3, 1795, Congress enacted the first legislation authorizing an official compilation of the laws. It directed the secretary of state to collect and to publish the compilation, and to include the text of the Constitution. It was issued in 1796 at public expense.

On April 18, 1814, Congress enacted a law authorizing the second official compilation of the laws. It thus was enacted when some of the Framers were still alive: Thomas Jefferson and John Adams died, by a remarkable coincidence, on the fiftieth anniversary of Independence, in 1826. The new official compilation was to be achieved by the attorney general. It was to include, in addition to the Constitution, as was authorized in the 1796 compilation, the Declaration of Independence and the Articles of Confederation. Prefacing this edition is an official letter from the attorney general, Richard Rush, to the secretary of state, James Monroe. The letter states a plan for the authorized compilation. Rush proposes, among other steps, to examine "the journals of the old congress," prior to 1789, so as to include "acts, ordinances, or resolutions" which "may serve to connect . . . the early official acts of the government, with the formation of the present constitution." Such materials are to be included in the first volume, along with the Declaration, the Articles and the Constitution, as stipulated by Congress. Monroe approved Rush's plan.

The Declaration of Independence is chapter 1 of the second official compilation of the laws. An explanatory note and a detailed chronology introduce the text of the Declaration. The note indicates that the chronology is supplied, "In order to mark the gradual approaches which the thirteen United States, when colonies, made to independence. . . ." The chronology—more than six rather closely printed pages—goes from September 1774 until July 4, 1776. It focuses almost entirely on "the principal measures taken by the delegates in congress," measures which at last culminated in the proclamation of the Declaration of Independence.

Immediately following the text of the Declaration is a note which says, in part: "It would seem that congress was, from the beginning, attentive to the commemoration of the declaration of independence." The note instances the resolution of June 24, 1778, by which "congress would, in a body, attend divine worship . . . to return thanks for the divine mercy, in supporting the independence of the states." The resolution also provides for the appointment of a committee of three who are to "take proper measures for a public celebration of the anniversary of independence."

Chronologies similar to that at the head of the Declaration preface the texts of the Articles of Confederation and the Constitution. Each reveals, early in our political history, a sense of the *continuity* of "the government" of the United States, from September 1774 right through to the commencement of the new federal government on March 4, 1789. And each reveals a sense of the intrinsic importance of each of the three documents to that continuity.

The third official compilation of the laws was authorized by a joint congressional resolution—which has the same legal status as an "act" of Congress—on March 3, 1845. The resolution directs the attorney general to contract with a commercial publisher, Little and

Brown, for copies of its "proposed edition of the Laws and Treaties of The United States." It also stipulates a number of conditions. Most important of these, for our inquiry, is this: "That the work shall contain the articles of Confederation, the Constitution, all the public and all the private laws. . . ." Later that year, *The Public Statutes at Large of the United States of America* (1845) was published. Its preface says, in part: "The edition of the Statutes of the United States presented to the public comprehends all the Public Acts passed since the organization of the government, preceded by the Declaration of Independence, the Articles of Confederation, and the Constitution of the United States."

Three things are worth noting about this third official compilation of the laws: First, the congressional resolution says nothing about including the Declaration of Independence. In fact, the placement of the Declaration as the first document in the volume seems to have a problematic legal basis. I have not been able to determine how and why it came to occupy the place of honor as the first document in the actual published work. But it is reasonable to conjecture that an editor at Little and Brown decided to include it, perhaps on the grounds that it was fitting that it be placed at the head of the fundamental documents of the Republic. It is also possible that he consulted both the 1814 legislation, which does stipulate the inclusion of the Declaration, as well as the 1814 edition of the laws, for in that edition, as we have seen, the very first document is the Declaration of Independence. Second, there is no general title for the section containing the three documents. Third, *The Statutes at Large* (1845) was the official version of the laws until it was superseded in 1875.

What we see, then, is that all during the growing sectional crisis that erupted in the Civil War, during the war itself, and during the greatest part of the era of Reconstruction—which is usually held to end in 1877, with the withdrawal of the last federal troops from the South—the 1845 version of *The Statutes at Large* was the authoritative one. And thus all during this critical period the *Statutes* of the

Republic are preceded, first and foremost, by the Declaration of Independence, with its ringing pronouncement of the principle that "all men are created equal." As we shall see presently, it is this principle upon which Abraham Lincoln will eventually take his stand in his unsuccessful bid to be elected to the Senate and then his successful bid to be elected president.

The next and decisive chapter in our story occurs during Reconstruction (1865–1877). By this time, a large body of laws had been passed since the issuance of the 1845 official version of the laws. Furthermore, the huge surge of legislative activity included the enactment of the Thirteenth Amendment, which ended slavery everywhere in the Union (1865); the Fourteenth Amendment, which bestowed citizenship on emancipated slaves (1868); and the Fifteenth Amendment, which gave them the right to vote (1870). It also included the enactment of sweeping laws giving statutory force to these Amendments. Congress accordingly felt obliged to readdress the problem of producing a new official version of the laws.

On June 27, 1866, under Andrew Johnson, who succeeded to the presidency after the assassination of Abraham Lincoln, Congress passed "An Act for the Revision and Consolidation of the Statute Laws of the United States." The president is authorized to appoint, by and with the consent of the Senate, three commissioners to "revise, simplify, arrange and consolidate all statutes of the United States, general and permanent in their nature, which shall be in force at the time such commissioners may make the final report of their doings." By this set of directives, Congress indicates the intention not just to bring the laws up to date, but to reduce them to a coherent and systematic form through the process technically known as codification. The commissioners are also required to present the revised statutes to the Congress so that they "may be re-enacted, if Congress shall so determine."

The work proved to be much more demanding than had been anticipated and there were changes in the membership of the commission. The commission's work was therefore extended three more years in an act passed May 4, 1870, during the presidency of Ulysses S. Grant. On March 3, 1873, Congress passed an act authorizing a joint committee to appoint a single commissioner to complete the work begun by the commission. The commissioner, Thomas Jefferson Durant, was a lawyer. His revised version of the laws was accepted by the joint committee, and then included in a bill enacted into law on June 24, 1874, and signed by President Grant. The crucial effect of this act was to codify all the statutes passed between 1789 and 1847 on the terms stipulated in the 1866 Act, and to repeal all the previous versions of statutes in the prior official compilations of the laws. This new official version of the statutes of the United States—the fourth such official version since the founding of the Republic—was called *The Revised Statutes of 1875*. It became the sole and authoritative positive, which is to say, fully enacted, law of the land. It is still, as of this writing, in 1998, the only compilation of the laws that has been fully so enacted.

The 1875 version, for reasons that remain as obscure as the reason why the Declaration of Independence was placed as the first document in the Statutes of 1845, did not contain any of the three fundamental documents that had graced the opening of the 1845 version. What is more, the 1875 version quickly proved to contain many inaccuracies and unauthorized versions of the laws. Consequently, in December 1876, just prior to the beginning of the presidency of Rutherford B. Hayes, a Special Committee of the Senate was appointed to consider further revision and republication of *The Revised Statutes of 1875*. The committee included George S. Boutwell, then a Republican senator from Massachusetts.

On January 12, 1877, Senator Allen G. Thurman (Dem.-Ohio) proposed that the new Revised Laws include the Articles of Confederation and the Constitution, a proposal that passed by unanimous consent. On February 14, 1877, an amendment to include the Declaration of Independence and the Ordinance of 1787 was proposed by the Boutwell committee and approved by the full Senate with little debate. On March 2, 1877, the full Congress passed an act authorizing the new president to appoint a single commissioner who was further to revise the statutes by bringing them up to date and by correcting the inaccuracies of *The Revised Statutes of 1875.*

A signal feature of the 1877 act, for our purposes, is the stipulation, which I have previously mentioned, that the commissioner is to include in the revised version "the Articles of Confederation, the Declaration of our National Independence, the Ordinance of seventeen hundred and eighty-seven for the government of the Northwestern Territory, the Constitution of the United States." Thus by act of Congress, not only are the three fundamental documents which preface the 1845 version of the laws to be restored to their place at the beginning of the laws of the Republic, but to them is to be added the Northwest Ordinance of 1787. I shall later have occasion to consider more fully the significance of this last addition. For now, it is sufficient to recall that that Ordinance, which came to have enormous effects on the settlement of the West, contained an explicit prohibition against the introduction of slavery into the area of the Northwest (Article the Sixth).

President Hayes appointed Mr. Boutwell, who had served on the Senate committee considering revision of *The Revised Statutes of 1875,* as the sole commissioner. Boutwell quickly completed his work, for in September 1878 he signed the preface to *The Revised Statutes of the United States, Second Edition, 1878.* In the preface, Boutwell calls attention to the stipulation of the 1877 statute that the four fundamental documents be included, and lists them in the order in which they are set down in the statute. But when we turn to the text of the new version we find that it begins with the four stipulated documents; that the section is titled "The Organic Laws of the United States"; and that now the Declaration of Independence has again become—as in 1845, and more remotely, in 1814—the first document.

I have been unable, in research at the National Archives, and in inquiries to the research division of the Library of Congress, to locate the working papers of Mr. Boutwell and any staff he may have employed, in order to determine exactly by whom and why the foregoing changes were made. But for reasons that will be set forth when I turn to a more detailed consideration of Mr. Boutwell and the political setting within which he did his work as commissioner, it is plausible to suggest that it was he who made them.

The Revised Statutes, Second Edition, 1878, was presented to the Congress, as had been the case with the 1875 version. But this time Congress, while "accepting" the corrected version, did not formally reenact the entire body of laws, as it had done in the Act of 1874 for the 1875 version. Nor has it since done so. In strict terms, then, Congress, while acknowledging Mr. Boutwell's revisions of the laws, did not formally enact the section titled "The Organic Laws of the United States." Its legal status remained that established in the key congressional act of 1877, and it remains so to this day, as we will now see.

After 1878, various attempts were made further to codify the laws, but none succeeded until the 1920s. During the interval, *The Revised Statutes, Second Edition,1878,* and the subsequent volumes of *The United States Statutes at Large,* which record chronologically all the acts and resolutions passed during a given session of Congress, constituted the official version of federal law, with the latter always controlling in case of a conflict between texts. The Organic Laws section of the 1878 official compilation thus continued to stand as a kind of preamble to the laws of the Republic all during the period from 1878 until well into the twentieth century.

One further chapter remains: In 1924, Congress authorized joint committees to develop a new codification of the laws—prospectively, the fifth official compilation since the beginning of the Republic. The work of the joint committees resulted in the first edition of *The United States Code,* published by the United States Government Printing Office and issued in 1926. Since then, a new edition has been issued approximately every six years. Although Congress has reenacted roughly half of the fifty titles contained in *The Code*, it has never reenacted the whole of the body of laws which have been passed since 1874 and which are still in force. The difficulties encountered with the 1875 version have had a surprisingly longterm effect.

The preface to the 1926 edition of *The United States Code* is of interest to our inquiry, for it begins as follows:

> This Code is the official restatement in convenient form of the general and permanent laws of the United States in force December 7, 1925, now scattered in 25 volumes—i.e., the Revised Statutes of 1875, and volumes 20–43, inclusive, of Statutes at Large. No new law is enacted and no law repealed. It is prima facie the law. It is presumed to be the law. The presumption is rebuttable by production of prior unrepealed Acts of Congress at variance with the Code. Because of such possibility of error in the Code and of appeal to the Revised Statutes and Statutes at Large, a table of statutes repealed prior to December 7, 1925, is published *together with the Articles of Confederation; The Declaration of Independence; Ordinance of 1787; the Constitution with amendments and index. . . .* The first official codification of the general and permanent laws of the United States was made in 1874 and followed by a perfected edition in 1878. (Emphasis added)

When we turn next to the table of contents of the first version of *The Code,* we find that there is a section titled ORGANIC LAWS OF THE UNITED STATES. It follows the "Text of Statutes," "Parallel Reference Tables," and "Table of Statutes Repealed Prior to December 7, 1925." There is no explanation why the text of the Organic Laws section has been displaced from its original position in *The Revised Statutes of 1875, Second Edition, 1878,* even though the 1926 preface cites the authority of that version. Nor is there any explanation why the order given in the 1926 preface is changed, such that, as in 1878, the Declaration of Independence comes first. Whatever the reasons for these changes, the Declaration has resumed what may arguably be called its privileged and rightful position.

A second edition of *The Code* was published in 1934. Now, the Organic Laws section is placed immediately before the "Text of Statutes." It thus resumes the place it had in 1878. In all the subsequent editions, it is the first section of *The Code*. And there it stands today, as a four-pillared porch onto the magisterial building which constitutes the "official" statement of "the General and Permanent laws of the United States."

That porch, it is now clear, is essentially what it was in the 1878 official version of the laws—except, of course, for the text of and the notes to all the Amendments which have been added to the Constitution since 1878. As for the historical notes appended to the text of the Declaration, the Articles, and the Constitution as it was in 1878, it is now worth noting their source. At the end of his preface to the 1878 edition of the laws, Boutwell says that the notes "are taken from a work entitled: 'The Organic Laws of the United States of America,' prepared by Maj. Ben. Perley Poore, and printed by authority of Congress." The full title to and the correct designation of the official basis of this work are as follows: *The Federal and State Constitutions, Colonial Charters, and other Organic Laws of the United States,* compiled under an order from the U.S. Senate by Ben. Perley Poore (Clerk of Printing Records), Washington: Government Printing Office, 1877. The notes which Boutwell added are thus part of a compilation ordered by the United States Senate. It is also noteworthy that the Poore volume refers generally to a variety of "organic laws" reflecting widespread usage of that terminology in the nineteenth century.

To sum up thus far: During nearly all of the time between 1814 and the present, the official body of federal laws has included, as the result of federal legislation, various of the four Organic Laws. Indeed, since 1878, with the brief exception of the period from 1926 to 1934, the section titled "The Organic Laws of the United States" has stood at the very head of our federal laws. And during most of the time from 1814 to the present, the Declaration of Independence has stood first in the Organic Laws section.

❁   ❁   ❁

What the present-day significance of this sketch of the history of the Organic Laws section may be is a large issue. For the question naturally arises as to the relationship of each of the four documents to the body of positive law in our own time, at the end of the twentieth century. What is certain, of course, is that the last of the four documents, the Constitution, has been "the supreme Law of the Land" (Art. VI, para. 2) ever since it was ratified by conventions of delegates chosen by the people of the various states and went into effect on March 4, 1789. How, though, to construe the inclusion of the Declaration and the Articles, since 1814, and those two plus the Northwest Ordinance of 1787, since 1878, as integral elements of "The Organic Laws of the United States"? And how to interpret their having been permitted to remain there ever since 1878?

Consider, first, the Articles of Confederation: It was superseded as the organizing document for the government of United States the moment the Constitution went into effect on March 4, 1789. Why, then, include it among "The Organic Laws of the United States"?

Consider, second, the Ordinance of 1787. It was enacted by the Congress under the Articles of Confederation. The First Congress under the new Constitution enacted the entire document, with a few necessary changes, as a law of the new Republic, on August 7, 1789. Thus one might argue that it was superseded as an "ordinance," just as its enacter, the Congress of the Articles of Confederation, was superseded, and that its measures for government of the Northwest Territory became simply part of the statute laws of the new United States of America. Why, then, should it have the august rank of an Organic Law?

Consider, third, and in some respects most critically, the case of the Declaration of Independence. It is neither "articles" nor "ordinance" nor "constitution" nor "law" in any ordinary sense of these terms. Indeed, strictly speaking, it does nothing but declare the independence of the thirteen United States from England. Yet it appears from 1814 to 1875, and then during most of the period from 1878 to the present, as the first of the documents which serve as a preamble to the laws of the Republic. Why should it be first among the Organic Laws?

To explore these questions properly it is necessary to turn from a narrow, if necessary, historical inquiry into the legislative basis of the Organic Laws section and to widen our horizon. We have to consider, first, the historical development of the terminology of political discourse in the American Republic; second, and more crucially, we must examine the remarkably charged political context within which "The Organic Laws of the United States" came to be the preamble to the laws of the Republic in 1878. That action occurs at the culmination of Reconstruction, which, in turn, was the culmination of the long struggle to end slavery as a legal institution—a struggle that was resolved, at last, only by a great Civil War. Herman Melville, at the end of *Battle-Pieces* (1866), echoing the slain Abraham Lincoln, called it "the terrible historic tragedy of our time" and prayed that "it may not have been enacted without instructing our whole beloved country through terror and pity." It is well, today, to recall this context for the emergence of the Organic Laws section of our federal statutes.

B. The Terminology of "Organic Laws" in the American Experience

Among the many remarkable features of the history of American constitutionalism are the range, the richness, and the subtlety of the terminology of political discourse to be remarked over the three centuries of its development. These qualities are perhaps nowhere more noticeable than in what Donald Lutz has called "the plethora of terms" that have been used by Americans to describe the nature of the political relationships, documents, and associations with which they have experimented ever since the first colonial settlements in the early seventeenth century.[15] Lutz calls attention to the importance, over time, of such diverse terms as these: "charter," "constitution," "patent," "agreement," "frame," "combination," "ordinance," and "fundamentals." He then shows how these are largely reducible to or capable of being ordered under four more general categories: "covenant," "compact," "contract," and "organic act." It is the last of these which is of greatest interest for our present inquiry.

Lutz bases his analysis on definitions in *The Oxford English Dictionary*, and on usage in scores of American governmental documents prior to and including the Constitution of 1789. Following his procedure, we find that *The Oxford English Dictionary* traces "organic" to a Greek root signifying "of or pertaining to an organ, instrumental." Definition 6b. reads: "Organizing, constitutive." The first quotation illustrating this usage is taken from the record of debates in the United States Congress, in 1849, then known as *The Congressional Globe*; it speaks of "the law of Congress" for organizing a "territory," and says that that law is "usually styled the 'organic law' establishing" the territory. An 1857 quotation refers to "the organic law, the charter"; and one from 1883 refers to "the organic Act" by which a "territory was organized."

Lutz, drawing on this definition in the *Oxford English Dictionary* and on a huge collection of historical materials, provides a useful definition of an "organic act." It is "one that codifies and celebrates an agreement or set of agreements made through the years by a community."[16] This sense of an "organic act" seems, on reflection, to fit well the character of the four varied documents which comprise "The Organic Laws of the United States." Thus a unanimous "declaration," a set of "articles" to form a "perpetual union," an "ordinance" setting forth principles to govern a vast new territory, and a "consti-

---

15. Donald S. Lutz, "From Covenant to Constitution in American Political Thought," *Publius,* Fall 1980, pp. 101–33. This entire article is a valuable source for understanding the terminology of the organic laws.

16. Ibid., p. 111.

tution" to organize a "more perfect Union" reveal progressively, between 1776 and 1789, the emergence of a new political community more and more rooted in fundamental agreements that are refined and strengthened over time. What is more, each of the four Organic Laws makes a distinctive contribution to that development, a contribution which citizens should come to understand as part of the meaning of the ultimate Organic Law, the Constitution.

This sense of the definitional fitness of the title, "The Organic Laws of the United States," is reinforced when we turn to examine the ready use of this terminology and an exploration of its meaning in the course of congressional debates during Reconstruction. Here are just a few examples.

On May 8, 1866, during debate on a proposed Fourteenth Amendment to the Constitution, Thaddeus Stevens, Radical Republican of Pennsylvania and House Chairman of the extraordinarily powerful Joint Committee on Reconstruction, made a long speech. He refers to the difficulty the committee has had in obtaining all "the *organic laws* and statutes" of the rebellious states. He then turns to the substance of the proposed Amendment. It would prohibit the states "from abridging the privileges and immunities of citizens of the United States"; further, it would prohibit the states from "unlawfully depriving" citizens of "life, liberty, or property," or "denying" to any of them the "'equal' protection of the laws." Stevens then characterizes the key provisions in these terms: "I can hardly believe that any person can be found who will not admit that every one of these provisions is just. They are all asserted, in some form or other, in our DECLARATION or *organic law*."[17]

On June 8, 1866, the Joint Committee on Reconstruction, which included Mr. Boutwell, then a member of the House of Representatives, recommended, in a joint resolution, a revised version of the proposed Fourteenth Amendment. The committee's conclusion

---

17. Alfred Avins, ed., *The Reconstruction Amendment Debates* (Richmond: Virginia Commission on Constitutional Government, 1967), p. 212. (Emphasis added)

states, in part, that the "so-called Confederate States are not, at present, entitled to representation" in the Congress; that before such representation can take place, there must be "adequate security for future peace and safety" in the states which had been at war with the Union; and that "this can only be found in such changes of the *organic law* [the Constitution] as shall determine the civil rights and privileges of all citizens in all parts of the republic."[18]

On March 31, 1871, James Monroe, a newly elected Republican representative from Ohio, made a speech on a proposed law to enforce the Fourteenth Amendment. His speech contains an analysis of the proper way for citizens and their legislators to reason on "constitutional" issues.[19] Monroe begins by contrasting what he calls the "logic of the popular mind and heart upon a constitutional question" with the kind of "logic" that "the courts" characteristically "approve." He comes down squarely on the side of the former, on the grounds that it most adequately grasps the nature of the Constitution. Monroe then advances two main principles of the proper way to interpret it. First, he asserts, "A constitution is a means and not an end." In explicating this principle, he refers to the Constitution as the "great *organic act*"[20] of a "free country"; he insists that the Framers, in constructing that organic act, did not "forget the foundations of society," above all the end of protecting the "life, liberty and property of the people"; he further insists that it is valid to presume that "such an instrument" contains "protection for the people"; and that in doubtful cases, where there may be "obscure or ambiguous phrases," it is proper to assume that such protection is intended to "give to the natural rights of man the benefit of the doubt." In so reasoning, it is clear that Monroe takes his stand ultimately on the principles of the Declaration of Independence, for it is the first of the Organic Laws, and then on the Constitution, for it is the ultimate Organic Law.

18. Ibid., p. 94. (Emphasis added)
19. Ibid., p. 514.
20. Ibid. (Emphasis added)

Monroe's second guiding principle is this: "To every free constitution there is a kind of natural growth." In explicating this principle, Monroe insists that such growth does not derive from "a change in the letter or spirit of the Constitution," nor from the "intrusion of new principles," but rather from the "more extended application of old ones," an application required by the advent of new and compelling "circumstances," including "new social conditions." He concedes that in the "application of a well-known principle" rooted in "the *organic law* of the land" to such new social conditions, the application may at first appear to some to be an unwarranted "innovation"; but it proves, on examination, to be "only the application of known and admitted principles to new circumstances." And then, in illustration of his argument, Monroe adduces, among other examples, President Lincoln's issuance of the Emancipation Proclamation on January 1, 1863. He insists that although many at first thought this action to be "unconstitutional," it "is now very generally approved"; and Monroe attributes that approval to a belated recognition that there was an application of the constitutional principle that there must be means for the end of the protection of "life, liberty and property." Thus Monroe once again links the principles of the Declaration to those of the Constitution, each an Organic Law, each having its place in ordering the frame of government.

The preceding examples of ready usage of the term "organic law" and "organic act" during congressional debates in the era of Reconstruction reflect a widespread understanding that the American Republic is, in fact, ordered by such laws—including, most fundamentally, as to the statement of the guiding principles, the Declaration of Independence. But to see just how deeply rooted that notion is in our constitutional history, it is necessary again to widen our horizon. To do this, we must consider the political setting which precedes and in crucial ways both informs and underlies the 1878 placement of the Organic Laws section at the head of the statutes of the Republic.

C. Political Reasoning on the Nature of the Organic Laws

> He has waged cruel war against human nature itself, violating its most sacred rights of life and liberty in the persons of a distant people who never offended him, captivating them & carrying them into slavery in another hemisphere, or to incur miserable death in their transportation thither. . . .

So begins a long passage in Thomas Jefferson's draft of the Declaration of Independence—a passage which, toward the end of the bill of particulars against King George III, charges him with abjectly refusing to bring an end to the "execrable commerce" in Negro slaves in the American colonies. The passage was expunged by Congress in the final version of the document, in good measure due to the objections of representatives from South Carolina and Georgia, but also due to the recognition, even by representatives from the northern states, that the slave trade was part of an institution already deeply rooted in America and on which many Americans were dependent.[21]

The tension between the original passage's vehement denunciation of the slave trade and Congress's action expunging it is deeply symbolic of the most profoundly troubling problem ever to afflict the American Republic—the problem of the existence of slavery in a nation which, at its founding, proudly declares: "We hold these truths to be self-evident, that all men are created equal. . . ." It is hardly surprising, then, as we shall now see, that each one of what will eventually be called "The Organic Laws of the United States" in 1878, in the wake of the Civil War, is very much implicated in and has reference to that most agonizing of constitutional problems.

---

21. See Dumas Malone, *The Story of the Declaration of Independence* (New York: Oxford University Press, 1954), pp. 75–77; Carl L. Becker, *The Declaration of Independence* (New York: Vintage Books, 1958).

I. Lincoln's Statesmanship

No American better understood the depth of the problem than did Abraham Lincoln. What is more, Lincoln's extraordinary mastery and rhetorical use of the fundamental documents of American constitutionalism provide a model for the appeal to such documents which marks the debates in Congress after the Civil War—debates that led up to and culminated in the placement of "The Organic Laws of the United States" as the preamble to the statute laws.

Lincoln's statesmanship is evident in many of his speeches. But for purposes of our inquiry, it is sufficient to focus on just three: his speech on the Supreme Court's *Dred Scott* Decision in 1857, his New York Cooper Institute speech during the presidential campaign in 1860, and his First Inaugural in 1861.

1. The Speech on the *Dred Scott* Decision.

The *Dred Scott* decision—the case officially is known as *Dred Scott* v. *Sanford*—was handed down by the Supreme Court on March 6, 1857. It has proved to be the most fateful, the most hotly debated, indeed the most explosive, decision yet made by the Court.[22]

The background to the decision is this: The prolonged sectional struggle between "free" states and "slave" states inevitably focussed on the huge, and potentially enormously wealthy, western territories that were progressively acquired by the original United States. The overriding question was simply this: As new states were formed in those territories, would they come into the Union as "free" or "slave"? Of crucial relevance to the *Dred Scott* decision was the Compromise of 1820—one of the great compromises which sought to provide a political answer to that question. At the time, there were eleven "free" states and eleven "slave." The key legislative part of the Compromise provided, first, that Maine

---

22. *Dred Scott* v. *Sanford,* 60 U.S. (19 Howard), 393 (1857).

would enter the Union as a "free" state and Missouri as a "slave" state; second, that all the huge western territory north of north latitude 36 degrees and 30 minutes, except for Missouri, would remain free of slavery.

Dred Scott, a slave, was taken in 1834 by his master from Missouri, a "slave" state, to Illinois, a "free" state, then to Wisconsin Territory, which was a "free" territory under the law of the Missouri Compromise, and then back to Missouri. In 1846, with the help of anti-slave lawyers, Scott sued for his freedom in a Missouri court on the grounds that his residence in Illinois and in Wisconsin Territory had made him free. He lost in the Missouri Supreme Court. The case at last reached the United States Supreme Court.

Roger B. Taney, the chief justice, wrote the majority opinion. But so contentious were the issues, and so portentous the outcome, that all of the other eight justices also wrote opinions, two of them dissenting from the holding of the majority opinion. The essence of Taney's ruling is reducible to two points: First, Scott was a slave not a citizen, and, being a Negro, could not be a citizen; hence he had no standing to sue in federal court. Second—and here lay the truly politically explosive finding—Congress had no power, in 1820, to exclude slavery from the territories; hence the provision of the Compromise of 1820 seeking to exclude it was unconstitutional. Henceforth, in effect, no attempt by Congress to prevent the expansion of slavery in the territories could be constitutional; and the nascent Republican party, which was dedicated above all to the prevention of that expansion, was for all practical purposes a nullity.

It is worth noting that this is only the second time in the history of the Republic that the Supreme Court had presumed to assert that an act of Congress was unconstitutional. To have done so with respect to a congressional act concerning the bitterly contested issue of the expansion of slavery into the territories was intended, in principle, forever to resolve that issue, on the premise that the Supreme Court is the final arbiter concerning the interpretation of the Constitution.

In fact, the storm of controversy unleashed by Taney's opinion helped prepare the way for the Civil War. An immensely important dimension of that controversy was the fact that Taney apparently felt obliged to include, as a key part of his opinion, an elaborately argued interpretation of the Founders' intention in enunciating the Declaration of Independence. The crux of his interpretation is this: The Declaration's ringing assertion of the "self-evident truth" that "all men are created equal" was understood by the Founders to apply only to white men and not to Negroes. And arguing from this crucial premise, Taney held that the Constitution itself, as understood by the Founders of '87, does not recognize any rights of Negroes that the white man must respect.

On December 10, 1856, shortly after James Buchanan, a Democrat, was elected president, and as the nation anxiously awaited the *Dred Scott* decision, Abraham Lincoln made a speech at a Republican banquet in Chicago. He said:

> Our government rests in public opinion. Whoever can change public opinion, can change the government, practically, just so much. Public opinion or [on?] any subject, always has a *"central idea,"* from which all its minor subjects radiate. That "central idea" in our political public opinion, at the beginning was, and until recently has continued to be, "the equality of men."[23]

Lincoln then asserts that the Democratic party, in the recent election campaign, sought to replace that old, fundamental central idea with its opposite—the "idea that slavery is right, in the abstract." He warns that if that effort should succeed, there is a real prospect that it would lay the moral foundation for "the perpetuity of slavery, and its extension to all countries and colors." Lincoln had in mind, among other things, the very real possibility that the Supreme Court, even then deliberating the *Dred Scott* decision, would lend its great

---

23. *The Collected Works of Abraham Lincoln,* Roy P. Basler, ed. (New Brunswick, N.J.: Rutgers University Press, 1953), II: 385. (Original emphasis)

weight to this new and dangerous "central idea." In so doing, it would help to bring about a decisive change in "public opinion."

When Taney's majority opinion more than confirmed Lincoln's fears, he began a relentless campaign of speeches to contest the issue, above all with Stephen Douglas, the Democratic senator from Illinois, who had adopted the principle of "popular sovereignty" on the issue of the expansion of slavery in the territories and who supported Taney's opinion. By this principle Douglas meant the right of the majority to decide whether to permit or to exclude slavery, thus, in Lincoln's judgment, ignoring the fundamental question of the moral rightness of slavery.

Lincoln delivered the first such speech in his home town of Springfield, Illinois, on June 26, 1857. His treatment of the *Dred Scott* decision focuses on two crucial points: First, what is the proper response to such a decision by the Supreme Court? Second, what are the historical facts with respect to the Declaration of Independence and its relationship to the Constitution?

On the first question, Lincoln begins by distinguishing between what he calls two "uses" of "judicial decisions": to determine the outcome of the immediate case before the court, and to "indicate to the public how other similar cases will be decided." The latter use is known as a "precedent" or "authority." Lincoln fully recognizes that "precedents" may and even should "control" the "general policy of the country," but adds the significant caveat that this is so only "according to circumstances." What, then, are the relevant circumstances regarding the enormously important *Dred Scott* decision?

Lincoln casts his argument in terms of a whole series of five very big "ifs," or conditionals. The first is this: "If this important decision had been made by the unanimous concurrence of the judges. . . ." Lincoln thus begins from a condition which he, his audience, and the citizens at large know not to have been met. In so doing, he rhetorically weights the consideration of the "circumstances" in favor of evidence which is readily available, incontestable, and undercuts the decision's claim to be a binding "precedent." As Lincoln proceeds, he enters more difficult terrain. For example, he specifies, as the third conditional, that the decision could claim to be a proper "precedent" if it had been made "in accordance with legal public expectation." What exactly Lincoln means by this phrase is surely more difficult to know than is the case with the first conditional, and the nature of such "public expectation" is surely also open to dispute. Even so, Lincoln appears to feel it is important to direct citizen attention to this area of constitutional interpretation as he builds the case against the claim of the decision to be a "precedent." Lincoln's fourth conditional is that the decision would be a "precedent" if it "had been in *no part,* based on *assumed* historical facts which are not really true" (emphasis added).

Not surprisingly, it is this particular conditional to which Lincoln soon turns in his elaboration of the reasons why the decision is not a proper "precedent." For by setting the true historical facts over against those which are counterfeit, but which seek to bolster the authority of the decision, he can lend support to the old and true "central idea" of our "political public opinion," the idea that undergirds the Republic: "the equality of men."

Lincoln prefaces his treatment of the true historical facts with a restatement of the first issue between him and Chief Justice Taney. He says that Taney, "in delivering the opinion of the majority of the Court, insists at great length that negroes were no part of the people who made, or for whom was made, the Declaration of Independence, or the Constitution of the United States." Lincoln then rebuts Taney, as to the Constitution, by drawing on historical evidence adduced in the dissenting opinion of Justice Curtis. The evidence is that in five states "free negroes" were "voters" at the time of the vote on ratification of the Constitution in 1787–88. Lincoln thus insists on extending the sense of the government back beyond the Constitution itself to the act of ratifying the newest form of constituting the government.

Lincoln then turns to the crucial question: Whether the Founders

understood the Declaration to apply to Negroes? Taney, taking
refuge in what may be called an "historicist" reading of the Declaration, asserts that the Founders, like other men in "the civilized and
enlightened portion of the world" at the end of the eighteenth century, necessarily believed Negroes to be *naturally* inferior to white
men, hence necessarily incapable of being included in the phrase
"all men are created equal" and thereby incapable of being members
of the political community. Taney, Lincoln says, further argues "that
the authors of that instrument did not intend to include negroes, by
the fact that they did not at once, actually place them on an equality
with whites." Lincoln's lengthy reply to this facet of Taney's argument is one of his most important statements interpreting the
meaning and application of the Declaration. It says, in part:

> I think the authors of that notable instrument intended to include
> *all* men, but they did not intend to declare all men equal *in all
> respects.* They did not mean to say all were equal in color, size,
> intellect, moral developments, or social capacity. They defined
> with tolerable distinctness, in what respects they did consider all
> men created equal—equal in certain "inalienable rights, among
> which are life, liberty, and the pursuit of happiness." This they
> said, and this meant. . . . They meant to set up a standard maxim
> for free society, which should be familiar to all, and revered by
> all. . . . Its authors meant it to be, thank God, it is now proving
> itself, a stumbling block to those who in after times might seek to
> turn a free people back into the hateful paths of despotism.[24]

Lincoln surely intends with this statement—and with many
similar ones he made as the crisis deepened—to show the inextricable linkage between the Declaration of Independence and the
Constitution, and to build into that linkage the essential premise,
the "central idea," of "the equality of men." Notice, too, his emphasis on making the key phrase from the Declaration a "standard

---

24. Ibid., II: 405–406. (Original emphasis)

maxim," which should be "revered by all." What is more, in a later part of the speech at Springfield, he sets up a mocking contrast between his interpretation of the Declaration and that of Taney-Douglas. According to the latter, that instrument was simply a justification by white British subjects in America for declaring independence from white British rule. Having obtained this end some eighty years ago, the Declaration is, according to Taney-Douglas, in Lincoln's mocking words, "of no practical use now—mere rubbish—old wadding left to rot on the battlefield after the victory is won." So regarded, the Declaration becomes "no more at most, than an interesting memorial of the dead past"; it is "shorn of its vitality, and practical value"; it is "left without the *germ* or even the *suggestion* of the individual rights of man in it."[25]

We will see the longterm and powerful effects of Lincoln's rhetoric concerning the nature and purpose of the Declaration when we turn, presently, to some of the congressional debates during Reconstruction. For now, it is sufficient to note that Lincoln rests his argument for the inextricable linkage of the Declaration and the Constitution not on any legislative enactments, such as the Congressional Act of 1845, which includes the Declaration, the Articles of Confederation, and the Constitution in the official compilation of the laws—as he might well have done—but on the far deeper stratum of the political and moral history of American constitutionalism. Without explicitly using here the terminology of "organic laws," Lincoln speaks the sense of that concept, not least in insisting that the Declaration's statement of principles was meant to have and continues to have, long after the Founding, immense "vitality" and "practical value."[26]

---

25. Ibid., II: 407. (Original emphasis)

26. For a thoughtful treatment of Lincoln's interpretation and use of the Declaration of Independence, see Harry V. Jaffa, "The Universal Meaning of the Declaration of Independence," chapter 14 of *The Crisis of the House Divided* (Garden City, N.Y.: Doubleday & Co., 1959), pp. 308–29.

2. The Cooper Institute Speech[27]

During his campaign for the presidency, Lincoln made a major speech, on February 27, 1860, at the Cooper Institute in New York City. The speech is, I suspect, the most extraordinary campaign speech ever uttered in America; indeed, when judged against campaign speeches of our times, it is truly astounding. For it joins a deeply learned inquiry into the early political history of the Republic to rhetorically eloquent appeals to the reason, good sense, sense of justice, patriotism, and magnanimity of his fellow citizens, south and north. As the tensions mount between North and South, Lincoln seeks to prevent a rupture of cataclysmic proportions and yet to insist upon maintaining the integrity of the central idea of the nation.

The question Lincoln addresses is this: "Does the proper division of local from federal authority, or anything in the Constitution, forbid *our Federal Government* to control as to slavery in *our Federal Territories*?"[28] He divides the speech into two parts. In the first part, he establishes, through meticulous historical analysis, that a majority of "the fathers" of the Republic who acted on the question voted in favor of such authority on a number of occasions. In the second part, he speaks, by turns, to "southerners" and "Republicans." For our purposes, it is the first part of the speech to which we will pay greater attention.

Lincoln's rhetorical strategy in his historical analysis is to focus on legislative actions of "the fathers," thirty-nine in number, who signed the original Constitution in 1787. (The names of the thirty-nine are appended to the text of the original part of the Constitution in this book.) He follows their official actions from the period of the nation under the Articles of Confederation all the way through the period of the passage of the Missouri Compromise of 1820. Lincoln's masterly summary of the historical record, we will now see,

---

27. *Collected Works,* III: 522–50.
28. Ibid., III: 523. (Original emphasis)

treats the Articles of Confederation, the Northwest Ordinance of 1787, and the Constitution as a series of inextricably connected measures bearing on the contested question of the authority of Congress to "control as to slavery in the territories." He does not explicitly refer to the Declaration of Independence in this historical analysis because his focus is on *legislative* actions taken by various of "the fathers" *after* the establishment of the independence of the American nation. But undergirding Lincoln's whole argument clearly is the position he took, in 1857, in the speech on the *Dred Scott* decision, asserting the continued "vitality" and "practical value" of the Declaration's ringing affirmation of the "self-evident truth" that "all men are created equal." It is the rock-bottom principle of the nation and underlies the stance taken by twenty-one of "the fathers" who, at various times between 1784 and 1820, voted to control slavery in the territories.

Here is a summary of the dates and the legislative acts to which, according to Lincoln, a *majority* of various among "the fathers" voted "aye":

1784: Under the Articles of Confederation, the Congress deliberated a proposed land ordinance for the newly acquired Northwest Territory which contained a provision forbidding slavery there. The act did not pass, but some of the fathers voted for it. (Lincoln forbears to state, as he might have done, that the land ordinance, including the provision forbidding slavery, was proposed by Jefferson.)

1787: Under the Articles, the Congress passed the Northwest Ordinance, which contains, in Article VI, the key provision forbidding slavery in the Territory.

1789: During the First Congress under the Constitution the Northwest Ordinance was enacted into law, including the provision against slavery. Sixteen of the original "fathers" were in the Congress. The act passed both houses "without yeas and nays, which is equivalent to an unanimous passage." George Washington, the first president and the presiding officer of the Constitutional Convention, as well as a slave-owner from Virginia, approved and signed the legislation.

1789: Also in the First Congress, the proposed first ten Amendments were passed. Of great importance here are Article VI, which stipulates that no person shall be deprived of "life, liberty or property without due process of law," and Article X, which reserves powers not delegated to the United States to the states or to the people. These two Articles are important because those who contend that there is no power in the Constitution to control slavery in the territories appeal to them even more than to the body of the Constitution. But the historical record shows that in the same Congress, the provision against slavery in the Northwest Territory and the two Amendments in question passed, indicating that those of "the fathers" who voted in favor of all these measures saw no conflict between the two sets of provisions.

1798: Congress passed legislation organizing the Territory of Mississippi. The act prohibits bringing slaves into the territory from outside the United States, and specifies that any so brought become free.

1804: Congress passed legislation organizing territory acquired in the Louisiana Purchase of 1803. This legislation controlled slavery even more than that concerning Mississippi.

1819–20: Congress deliberated many measures, including, most particularly, the prohibition of slavery, and one of "the fathers" voted consistently for that prohibition.

In the latter part of his speech addressing "the Southern people," Lincoln deftly refers them to a letter written by George Washington to the Marquis de Lafayette a year after Washington retired from the presidency. Fastening on Washington's having "approved and signed" the law of 1789 enacting the Northwest Ordinance, with its provision prohibiting slavery in the territory, Lincoln says that Washington "wrote Lafayette that he considered that prohibition a wise measure, expressing in the same connection his hope that we should at some time have a confederacy of free States."[29] Appended as footnotes to the text of Lincoln's speech that was subsequently published as a pamphlet are thirty-nine elaborate annotations. These were prepared by Charles Nott and Cephas Brainerd, members of the Board of Control in New York. Lincoln thought the annotations "exceedingly valuable."[30] That comment is worth considering when one reads, in annotation number 26, these statements by Washington concerning the Northwest Ordinance's 1787 prohibition against slavery: "I have long considered [negro slavery] a most serious evil, both socially and politically. . . . [The prohibition against it in the Northwest Ordinance of 1787] meets with the approval and assent of nearly every member from the States more immediately interested in Slave labor. The prevailing opinion in Virginia is against the spread of slavery in our new territories, and I trust we shall have a confederation of free States."

One final point about this speech is greatly worth considering given our present circumstances. Having concluded his survey, Lincoln quite sensibly poses this question: Are we "bound to follow implicitly whatever our fathers did"? His answer is that we should not; for that would, in principle, reject "all the lights of current experience," "all progress," "all improvement." Yet, he continues, if we would "supplant the opinions and policy of our fathers," we must do so "upon evidence so conclusive, and arguments so clear, that even their great authority, fairly considered and weighed, cannot stand."[31] That is a remarkably rigorous test, one that many present-day jurists and scholars largely ignore, not least because they start from the premise that appeal to such "authority" is itself outmoded.

Lincoln's own perception of the immense weight properly to be given to the fundamental principles of "the fathers" is beautifully set forth in a fragmentary statement ascribed by Roy Basler, the

---

29. Ibid., III: 537.
30. Ibid., III: 521, fn. 1.
31. Ibid., III: 535.

editor of Lincoln's writings, to the period between the 1858 sena-
torial campaign and his inauguration in 1861. It is what Harry Jaffa
calls a "meditation" on Proverbs 25:11. The biblical verse is: "A
word fitly spoken is like apples of gold in pictures of silver." In
Lincoln's meditation, the Declaration's assertion that "all men are
created equal" is restated as "the principle of 'Liberty to all.' " Lincoln then analogizes the double image of the biblical verse to the
relationship of the two fundamental documents of American constitutionalism thus:

> The *expression* of that principle, in our Declaration of Indepen-
> dence, was most happy, and fortunate. . . . The assertion of that
> *principle*, at *that time*, was the word, *"fitly spoken"* which has
> proved an "apple of gold" to us. The *Union,* and the *Constitution,*
> are the *picture of silver,* subsequently framed around it. The pic-
> ture was made, not to *conceal,* or destroy the apple; but to *adorn,*
> and *preserve* it. The picture was made *for* the apple—*not* the
> apple for the picture.[32]

3. The First Inaugural[33]

When Lincoln took the oath of office on March 4, 1861, he perceived that he did so with only problematic help to be had from the
"precedent" of the deeds and words of his fifteen predecessors. For,
in contrast to them, he indicates, he enters the office "under great and
peculiar difficulties. A disruption of the Federal Union heretofore
only menaced, is now formidably attempted." The pressing and decisive question he had to address was the legitimacy of the southern
states' claim that they have a right to "secede" from the Union.

What, then, is the nature of the Union? Lincoln's answer rests
on two pillars: "universal law" and "the Constitution." By the first
he means the universal sense of what essentially belongs to the con-

---

32. Ibid., IV: 168. (Emphasis in original)
33. Ibid., IV: 262–71.

stituting of what he calls a "government proper." Any such government intends, by its very nature, to be "perpetual," and none "ever had a provision in its *organic law* for its own termination."[34] Lincoln, who once studied Euclid's geometry to sharpen his powers of reasoning, implicitly here reckons a proposition to include a provision for self-termination in a government's "organic law" to be a contradiction in terms, and, in practical terms, an absurdity.

Lincoln moves, next, from the core sense of "universal law" and "government proper," to the contention by southern states claiming the right to secede, that the Union is "but an association of States in the nature of contract merely." Lincoln's reply distinguishes two cases: First, a contract among several parties may be "violated" or "broken" by one—or more—of the parties who entered into it. In such a case, Lincoln implies, there is an act of injustice. Second, a contract may be "lawfully" rescinded, which is to say repealed or rendered void. But in this case, Lincoln argues, all who entered the contract must agree to rescind. Clearly, then, even if one were to accept the southern states' argument that the Union is but a "contract," they cannot *by themselves* lawfully rescind it.

Lincoln now "descends" from "general principles" concerning the nature of government to principles concerning the nature of the "Union" in relation to the nature of the Constitution. In this phase of his argument, he extends the historical horizon he used in the Cooper Institute speech. There he begins with the Articles of Confederation because they were the form of government of the United States which existed when the first key prohibition against the expansion of slavery into the territories was passed in 1787, and the legitimacy of that prohibition is his focus in the 1860 speech. In the First Inaugural, the larger question of the very nature of the Union occupies the center of Lincoln's attention.

Lincoln now flatly asserts his fundamental premise: "The

---

34. Ibid., IV: 264. (Emphasis added)

Union is much older than the Constitution." He then begins to mount the evidence for this assertion from what is the first public act forming the Union—"the Articles of Association in 1774." He next moves quickly to the Declaration of Independence in 1776, which "matured and confirmed" the Union instituted in 1774. Four years later came the Articles of Confederation of 1778, by which the Union was "further matured" and "the faith of all the then thirteen States" was "expressly plighted and engaged that it should be perpetual." With this assertion, Lincoln invokes four passages in the Articles: Early in the text, the thirteen states title their action "Articles of Confederation and perpetual Union. . . ." Then near the end of the document, Article XIII thrice specifies that the Articles establish a Union which "shall be perpetual."

Lincoln finally arrives at the Constitution of 1787 and observes that "one of the declared objects for ordaining and establishing the Constitution, was *to form a more perfect union.*"[35] In so doing, Lincoln invokes the first of the ends set forth in the Preamble to the Constitution. From his perspective, that part of the Constitution is as valid, in revealing the nature of the government and the Union, as the rest of the instrument. In so holding, Lincoln in effect echoes the perspective of Story, as we have seen in considering his *Commentaries on the Constitution.*

Having thus in very short compass reviewed the principal actions of the people's representatives, from 1774 to 1787, Lincoln is now ready to draw conclusions from what might be called his political geometry: First, if it should be granted that one of the states, or even a group of states, may *lawfully* leave the Union, this would be to render the Union "*less* perfect than before the Constitution, [it] having lost the vital element of perpetuity." But this is in contradiction to the original intention of all the parties to form a perpetual Union. Second, "*resolves* and *ordinances*" seeking to effect secession being unlawful, the only alternative, "acts of vio-

---

35. Ibid., IV: 265. (Original emphasis)

lence . . . against the authority of the United States are insurrectionary or revolutionary, according to circumstances."[36]

The question naturally arises which of these alternatives may be in prospect. Now whether the southern states have legitimate grounds to appeal to the "right of revolution" depends, precisely, on what Lincoln laconically calls the "circumstances." And that they have no such grounds is set forth in a good portion of the remainder of the First Inaugural. Lincoln argues, in part, as follows:

> Think, if you can, of a single instance in which a plainly written provision of the Constitution, has been denied? If, by the mere force of numbers, a majority should deprive a minority of any clearly written constitutional right, it might, in a moral point of view, justify revolution—certainly would, if such right were a vital one. But such is not our case. All the vital rights of minorities, and of individuals, are so plainly assured to them, by affirmations and negations, guaranties and prohibitions, in the Constitution, that controversies never arise concerning them. But no *organic law* can ever be framed with a provision specifically applicable to every question which might occur in practical administration.[37]

Lincoln's characterization of the Constitution as the "organic law" in this passage reminds us of his earlier use, in this same speech, to refer more generally to the nature of those instruments which give constitutional form to "government proper." And the line of argument advanced in the First Inaugural concerning the progression and linkage of fundamental acts culminating in the Constitution reminds us of parallel lines of argument in the speeches on the *Dred Scott* decision and at the Cooper Institute. Once again, that is, the sense of inextricably linked "organic acts" is present; but in each case it is adjusted to the circumstances Lincoln is addressing.

---

36. Ibid., IV: 253. (Original emphasis)
37. Ibid., IV: 267. (Emphasis added)

We must next see how this sense of linked "organic acts" informs many of the crucial debates in Congress during the era of Reconstruction and underlies the placement of the Organic Laws section as the preamble to the statute laws in 1878.

II. Congressional Debates in the Nineteenth Century,
and Especially the Era of Reconstruction, 1865–1875

In 1967, the Virginia Commission on Constitutional Government published *The Reconstruction Amendments' Debates: The Legislative History and Contemporary Debates in Congress on the 13th, 14th, and 15th Amendments,* edited by Alfred Avins. This valuable volume brings together some two thousand pages of debates which took place in Congress during the first critical decade after the Civil War. At issue, among Republicans as well as between Republicans and Democrats, were great and greatly troubling questions concerning the meaning and the reach of the United States Constitution, questions that had vexed the nation for decades prior and during the Civil War, and which continue to vex it to this day. Perusal of the index of the Avins volume shows that among the subjects very frequently considered were these: "bill of rights," "citizenship," "civil rights," "discrimination by law," "due process," "education," "equal protection," "equality before the law," "natural rights," "privileges and immunities," "property," "republican form of government," "right to hold office," "schools," "slavery," "social equality," "states' rights," and "voting."

Perusal of the index also shows that at least two hundred—or about one-tenth of the pages—of the debates include explicit references to the Declaration of Independence. When one surveys the texts of the debates, one finds, in addition, scores of other pages which contain tacit references to that document in arguments concerning "natural rights" or "inalienable rights" or "civil rights." It is thus perfectly evident, from a perusal of these hundreds of pages, that apart from the Constitution itself, no single other document of our constitutional history so informs the congressional exchanges as does the Declaration. What is more, as one reads these portions of the debates, one is struck, again and again, with the sense that the principles of the Declaration are the ultimate standard for the law on fundamental matters of rights, even though there is understandably disagreement—sometimes wide disagreement—on the exact sense of the detailed application of the principles to the particulars of legislation.

There is no entry in the index for the Articles of Confederation as such; but a survey shows, as we shall presently see, the continuing importance of that document in arguments concerning, for example, the "privileges and immunities" of "citizens" and in citations of congressional authority, under the Articles, for the passage of the Northwest Ordinance.

As for the Ordinance itself, the index directs attention to a dozen or so places where it is explicitly treated. Here again a survey shows, as we shall also presently see, a persistent emphasis on its extraordinary importance in having prohibited the establishment of slavery in the territories.

Let us examine, then, just a few examples from among the many that could be cited of how the debates articulate appeals to one or the other of those three "organic laws" which precede the Constitution in time yet which are held to exert a continuing influence upon its meaning and reach.

1. The Declaration of Independence

The Thirty-ninth Congress was the first to convene after the Civil War. Shortly before it convened, in December 1865, Schuyler Colfax, a Republican from Indiana and the Speaker of the House of Representatives, made a speech outlining the Republicans' objectives. Colfax gives a very broad statement of the scope of the Republicans' commitment: they intend to guarantee, through federal legislation and federal enforcement, the civil rights not just of the freed slaves, but of all Americans: "[T]he Declaration of Independence must be recognized as the law of the land, and *every man, alien and native, white and black,* protected in the inalienable and God-given rights of life, liberty, and the pursuit of happiness."[38] Colfax further argues that the Republicans, in so acting, are but following the policy of Lincoln, who not only began the freeing of the slaves with the Emancipation Proclamation in 1863, but promised that the federal government would effectively maintain that freedom.

Early in the Thirty-ninth Congress, the Republicans introduced a civil rights bill. It was intended to carry out the sweeping purpose stated by Colfax, and to give effective force of statute law to the emancipation of the Negro slaves effected by the Thirteenth Amendment, which became the law of the land in December 1865. In defending the bill, Senator Lyman Trumbull of Illinois argues that the rights it guarantees to every citizen are "those inherent, fundamental rights which belong to free citizens or free men in all countries." He then asserts that these rights "are known as natural rights," and supports this view by appealing to the authority of William Blackstone and James Kent. Trumbull quotes Kent—who is frequently cited as an authority in the Reconstruction debates— to this effect:

> The absolute rights of individuals may be resolved into the right of personal security, the right of personal liberty, and the right to acquire and enjoy property. These rights have been justly considered, and frequently declared, by the people of this country to be natural, inherent and inalienable.[39]

Trumbull adduces as further support for his view a statement by President Johnson, in his annual message to Congress: "The Amer-

---

38. Quoted in Robert J. Kaczorowski, "Revolutionary Constitutionalism in the Era of the Civil War and Reconstruction," *New York University Law Review* 61 (November 1986): 894. (Original emphasis)

39. Avins, *The Reconstruction Amendment Debates,* p. 197.

ican system rests on the assertion of the *equal* right of every man to life, liberty and the pursuit of happiness."[40]

In the House of Representatives, William Lawrence (Rep.-Ohio) gave a lengthy and learned speech in defense of the civil rights bill. Lawrence had been a state judge and the editor of *Western Law Monthly* prior to his service in the Congress. Alfred Avins, who studied the entire body of debates, judges that Lawrence's speech is the "best exposition of Republican legal theories" in support of the bill. Lawrence's speech is therefore particularly useful for our inquiry.[41]

Lawrence's basic premise concerns the essence of the legislative power in the American form of government. He says: "Legislative powers exist in our system to protect, not to destroy, the inalienable rights of men." He first adduces as support for this premise several authorities: learned commentaries on the Constitution and judicial opinions. He next turns to a line of argument remarkably similar to that employed by Lincoln in the First Inaugural. Thus Lawrence begins an historical excursus with the Declaration of Rights of the Continental Congress of 1774, which says, in part, "That the inhabitants of the English colonies of North America, by the immutable laws of nature, the principles of the English constitution, and the several charters or compacts," have the right to "life, liberty and property." Lawrence next proceeds to quote the statement of principles of the Declaration of Independence, "That all men are created equal." He follows this with a partial quotation of the Preamble to the Constitution: "Promote the general welfare and secure the blessings of liberty"; with the citation of several more legal authorities; and with a conclusion which quotes the key portion of the Fifth Amendment to the Constitution: "No person . . . shall be deprived of life, liberty, or property without due process of law."

---

40. Ibid. (Original emphasis)
41. Ibid., pp. 205–206.

Lawrence sums up his historical excursus and citation of learned authority thus:

> It has never been deemed necessary to enact in any constitution or law that citizens should have the right to life or liberty or the right to acquire property. These rights are recognized by the Constitution as existing anterior to and independently of all laws and all constitutions.

They exist, as the Declaration asserts, as "self-evident truths" and according to the "laws of nature and of nature's God." They exist, in Lawrence's view, eighty years or so after they were first enunciated, as a continuing source of legitimacy for the activity of government.

2. The Articles of Confederation

Some of the most prolonged and contentious debates between 1865 and 1875 concerned the precise sense and implications of the phrase "privileges and/or immunities of citizens." Indeed, roughly six hundred pages of the debates contain some reference to the issue, often in great detail.

The issue focuses on the connection among three closely related sets of texts: Article IV of The Articles of Confederation ("the free inhabitants of each of these States . . . shall be entitled to all privileges and immunities of free citizens in the several States"); Article IV, Section 2 of the Constitution ("The citizens of each State shall be entitled to all Privileges and Immunities of Citizens in the several States"); and a draft of Section 1 of the proposed Fourteenth Amendment ("No State shall make or enforce any law which shall abridge the privileges or immunities of citizens of the United States").

It is obvious that each of the three documents employs very similar terminology. What is not at all obvious, however, is what

each of the key terms—"privileges," "immunities," "citizens"—
means, and whether the same term in the different documents has
the same intention. At stake, for example, is the definition of what
a "citizen" is, and which level of government determines the scope
of "citizenship," or what the relationship is between "rights of citizenship" and "rights of man," let alone what kinds of "privileges"
or "immunities" pertain to "citizens" within the states or as "citizens" of "the United States."

In an attempt to clarify the issue, a number of senators and members of the House of Representatives often turned back to the Articles of Confederation as the precursor to the Constitution. Thus, for
example, Senator Vickers (Dem.-Maryland) argues that the phrase
"privileges and immunities" was deliberately transferred from the
Articles of Confederation to the Constitution, but the "reasons"
given in the Articles—"the better to secure mutual friendship and
intercourse among the people of the different States"—were omitted
because the entire object of the Constitution was to promote these
ends. He goes on to argue that the only "privileges and immunities"
so transferred were those intended under the Articles of Confederation: "They cannot therefore be larger or more extensive in the Constitution in their construction and definition than they were under the
confederation." Vickers's object is to restrict the rights in question
to the basic enjoyment of "life, liberty, and property."[42]

A still more revealing and significant return to the Articles concerns the little phrase "free inhabitants" in Article IV of that document. A number of speakers in the Reconstruction debates call
attention to a key vote in the Congress deliberating on the content
of the Articles on June 25, 1778. The debate concerned a motion by
the delegation from South Carolina to insert the word "white" after
the word "free," thus restricting any "privileges and immunities" to
"free *white* inhabitants." Senator John Henderson (Rep.-Missouri)
cites the fact that the vote was eight states against the amendment,

---

42. Ibid., pp. 626–27.

two for, and one divided. He concludes: "This proves beyond doubt that the privileges and immunities of citizenship were at that time willingly accorded to all men who were free, who were not slaves, whether white or black."[43] The significance is that there is a continuity of the meaning of the constitutional regime from the Articles to the Constitution, a sense of continuity which echoes that posited by Lincoln in the various speeches we have had occasion to consider. And thus the Articles, though less significant than the Declaration of Independence in delineating the character of American constitutionalism, are nonetheless part of that development.

3. The Northwest Ordinance of 1787

In 1856, as the sectional crisis deepened, Edward Coles, a Virginian who had become governor of Illinois in the 1820s, read a paper before the Historical Society of Pennsylvania. He argued that Thomas Jefferson, a fellow Virginian and the principal author of the Declaration of Independence, was also the "enlightened and benevolent author" of the Northwest Ordinance of 1787. He based this claim largely on the fact that Jefferson, as a member of Congress, had proposed, in 1784, a land ordinance which prohibited slavery in the territories to be acquired by the cession to the United States of huge tracts of land from states such as Virginia. Although, in fact, that ordinance narrowly failed to pass, and although Jefferson was in France when the Northwest Ordinance did pass in 1787, public arguments such as those by Coles, Lincoln, and many others had the effect of making the Ordinance become widely known as "Mr. Jefferson's Ordinance" or "The Jeffersonian Ordinance."[44]

This sense of the Ordinance, and what is more, the sense of it as a still operative and guiding document of the Republic, appears

---

43. Ibid., p. 234.

44. See Peter S. Onuf, *Statehood and Union: A History of the Northwest Ordinance* (Bloomington & Indianapolis: Indiana University Press, 1987), pp. 144–45; Jaffa, *The Crisis of the House Divided,* p. 143.

in a number of places in congressional debates just prior to the Civil War, during the war, and during Reconstruction. Thus in 1859, in debates on the admission of Oregon as a state, one great issue was the legality, let alone the moral propriety, of Section 4 of the Oregon constitution. That section provides that "No free negro or mulatto" not "residing" in the state at the time of the adoption of the state constitution "shall ever come, reside, or be within this State, or hold any real estate, or make any contract, or maintain any suit therein." John Bingham, Republican member of the House of Representatives from Ohio, who was to be a member of the crucial Joint Committee on Reconstruction in the Thirty-ninth Congress after the Civil War, vehemently characterizes the section as an "infamous atrocity." He asserts that it flatly violates key provisions of "the ordinance of 1787," which, by an Act of Congress in 1848, was extended to apply to Oregon. In particular, it violates Article II of the Ordinance. That Article stipulates that inhabitants of a territory are "entitled to the benefits of the writs of habeas corpus," the right to "trial by jury," and the right to make and enforce "private contracts."[45]

In April 1862, a year after the Civil War began, Mr. Bingham, in a speech concerning a proposed act for emancipation of slaves in the District of Columbia, says this: "Happily the language of this bill, forever prohibiting slavery here, is the very language of one of the first enactments of Congress under the Constitution of the United States"—the Act of August 7, 1789, by which the Ordinance became positive law of the new Republic. Bingham goes on to characterize that "legislation" as "the law of liberty of all the Territories" and an acknowledgment, because of Article VI's prohibition of slavery, of "the great truth that 'all men are created equal' . . . in respect to those rights which are as universal as the material structure of man."[46]

In 1865, the language of Article VI of the Ordinance was in

---

45. Avins, *The Reconstruction Amendment Debates,* p. 17.
46. Ibid., p. 38.

large part that of the proposed Thirteenth Amendment. In 1866, in debates on the Freedmen's Bureau Bill for the protection and aid of the emancipated slaves, Representative Ignatius Donnelly (Rep.-Minnesota) spoke—as did many in the Reconstruction Congresses—of "Jefferson's famous ordinance, which gave to freedom the Northwestern Territory."[47] Although as we near the end of the twentieth century few citizens probably are much aware of this sense of the importance of the Northwest Ordinance, it remains where men like George Boutwell saw fit to put it, among our Organic Laws.

Boutwell was remarkably articulate, when in Congress, concerning the Fourteenth and Fifteenth Amendments and an enabling 1875 Civil Rights Bill. Some of his remarks in the Senate in May 1874 are particularly revealing of his perspective on the nature of the American regime in the aftermath of the Civil War. The immediate question being debated was a hotly disputed one: whether the civil rights law could constitutionally prohibit public schools to segregate students by race or color. Here is part of what Boutwell said:

> I wish to break down the prejudice in the public mind by which it is possible in some cities and sections of the country to make separate schools and give to children, who when they become men are bound by the same political bonds to a government based upon the doctrine of equality, ideas which are inconsistent with the existence of such institutions; for it is only by instilling into the minds of the children and the youth of the country the idea that there is no difference by nature or birth or caste, that we can take security for the continuance of the institutions under which we live . . . nothing is right but absolute equality of rights.[48]

It is hardly surprising, in the light of such a statement, that Boutwell should have been one of those, in 1877, to propose the

---

47. Ibid. p. 136.
48. Ibid., p. 703.

inclusion of the Declaration of Independence and the Northwest Ordinance in the group of fundamental documents to be included in the revised edition of the statute laws. Nor is it surprising, given the extent to which the concept of "organic laws" permeates congressional debates in the Reconstruction era, that he should have thought it fitting to title the entire body of fundamental laws "The Organic Laws of the United States."

CONSTITUTIONAL RESTORATION

I began this Introduction by briefly contrasting Lincoln's and Brennan's understandings of the Constitution. In light of the inquiries I have now made, it is fitting to reflect a bit further on that contrast.

Lincoln's understanding of the Constitution as *the organic law* of the government and the nation reflects a widespread general sense, in the nineteenth century, that there is a large body of such organic laws in America; that, so far as the national government is concerned, the Declaration of Independence and the Constitution are enduring and fundamentally harmonious; and that the Articles of Confederation and Northwest Ordinance are contributory to the making of the American Republic.

But it was Lincoln who most perceptively seized upon the sense of the importance of Organic Laws in American political discourse, and who sought, through rhetorically powerful speeches, to make an understanding of them a bedrock stratum of "political public opinion." In those speeches—only three of which I have been able to treat here—Lincoln manifests a profound reverence for the Constitution as *the* ultimate organic law of the nation. That reverence, in turn, is rooted in searching analysis of and reflection on the Constitution as the formal embodiment of the principles of the great anterior founding organic law, the Declaration of Independence.

Lincoln's public utterances on this theme are stunningly crystallized in his private meditation on Proverbs 25:11: He turns to the language of Scripture to formulate a lovely visual image of the "apple of gold," the *principle* that "all men are created equal," framed by the "picture of silver," the Union and the Constitution.

Lincoln's repeated use of the word *principle* in his meditation exemplifies his steadfast adherence to the way in which the Fathers thought and wrote. It reflects, that is, thoughtful acceptance of their understanding that there are fundamental beginning points of political inquiry; that these are truly *principles,* which is to say, knowable first things; that they are in principle knowable by every human being because they are rooted in nature and in teachings about nature; that they are, because so rooted, permanent; and that they provide the only true foundation for properly ordering government and its laws. Lincoln looks to beginnings, then, not out of any mere piety toward the Fathers, but because of a profound recognition that the principles they enunciated were and remain the true ones. To Lincoln, to make real progress in understanding fundamentals concerning government and law is actually to *return,* repeatedly, to analysis of and reflection on the Organic Laws.

Brennan's understanding of the Constitution, seen in this light, is ultimately irreconcilable with Lincoln's. Brennan surely pays genuine respect to the Framers, to the original Constitution, and to what he at times calls the fundamental principles of the Founding. But careful analysis of the whole of his 1985 speech indicates that underlying and informing his understanding is an unshakable conviction that enormous progress has been made in understanding the Constitution since 1787. Indeed, that conviction, although at times truly in tension with respect for the Constitution, in the end triumphs over it.

That triumph is emphatically revealed in the terminology Brennan most favors in treating the Constitution. His repeated characterizations of it as "a sublime oration on the dignity of man," as declaring "certain values transcendent," and as embodying great "political and legal ideals" or "substantive value choices," partake of fashionable political discourse of the latter part of the twentieth century. But all these are, I suggest, essentially anachronistic interpretive glosses imposed on the Constitution.

To put the matter in strictest terms, not one of these characterizations by Brennan has any direct foundation in the Constitution. Nor is his favorite expression, "human dignity," which he holds to be the supreme end of the Constitution (he uses the expression nearly thirty times in his speech), ever to be found in *The Federalist*, the most learned and detailed commentary on the Constitution at the time of the ratification debates. And the term "values," which Brennan so readily and apparently deliberately interchanges with "principles," probably because "values" is omnipresent in today's moral and political discourse, simply did not exist in its present sense at the time of the Founding. On the other hand, the term "principle" occurs over two hundred times in *The Federalist*, and it is that term which Lincoln so unerringly relies upon.

But the real issue is not that of anachronistic terminology. Rather, it is the validity of Brennan's two principles: First, that the meaning of the Constitution is itself ineluctably in constant evolution; and second, that it is the supreme and unique duty of the justices of the Supreme Court to discern that evolution and to instruct—to use Lincoln's phrase—"political public opinion" in the newer and newer meanings.

The citizen who has reached this point in my Introduction will certainly decide for himself or herself, as is fitting and indeed inevitable, whether my argument on behalf of the greater persuasiveness of Lincoln's understanding of the Constitution is convincing. The text of "The Organic Laws of the United States of America" is the indispensable primary material for making an independent judgment on the issue. But I also will suggest a few books which may prove helpful in the study of those texts and, more generally, in the study of themes touched on in this Introduction. The Suggested Reading at the end of the book provides a more extensive list.

The Federalist was written by Alexander Hamilton, John Jay, and James Madison but publicly presented as the work of Publius, a Latin name signifying a public-spirited citizen. It forthrightly champions the new Constitution and urges Publius's fellow citizens to ratify it. It is the most influential analysis of and commentary on the Constitution ever to be published. An 1825 Resolution of the Board of Visitors of the University of Virginia, of which Thomas Jefferson was rector, states that *The Federalist* is an "authority" on "questions" as to "the genuine meaning" of the Constitution. It is readily available in various inexpensive paperback editions.

The Federalist states and seeks to refute the main criticisms of the proposed new Constitution which were set forth by the "Anti-Federalists." But it is useful, even today, to revisit the main arguments of the opposition as they are presented by the critics themselves. A useful introduction to those writings is Herbert J. Storing's *What the Anti-Federalists Were For.* Storing rightly argues that those patriotic critics made an important contribution to "the dialogue of the American founding." He further argues that, because the political life of the nation "continues to be a dialogue . . . the Anti-Federalist concerns and principles still play an important part."[49] Current dialogues on the nature of "rights" and on the proper relationship of the federal to state governments are but two obvious examples where revisiting both Federalist and Anti-Federalist arguments is worthwhile.

A treasure house of documents from the era of the Founding is *The Founder's Constitution: Major Themes*, volume I of a five-volume set edited by Philip B. Kurland and Ralph Lerner.

Two books by George Anastaplo are exemplary: *The Constitution of 1787: A Commentary*, and *Amendments to the Constitution: A Commentary.* These books have two great virtues: First, they treat the Constitution as a coherent whole whose parts throw light upon each other and thus require careful, sustained study. Second, they

---

49. Herbert J. Storing, *What the Anti-Federalists Were For* (Chicago: The University of Chicago Press, 1981), p. 3.

are clearly written and are largely directed to the general reader and citizen. They provide splendid examples of how to go about the study of each of the Organic Laws, and give a detailed interpretation of the Constitution and its Amendments.

Harvey Mansfield's *America's Constitutional Soul* is a collection of essays setting forth "a constitutional view of American politics." The Introduction ("Political Science and the Constitution") and the essays in Parts III ("Constitutional Origins") and IV ("Constitutional Forms"), in particular, are thoughtful contributions to a project of constitutional restoration, for they are wide-ranging reflections on the nature of the Constitution and on present-day influential doctrines that impede its careful study.

The relationship between moral principles and the Constitution is a problem as old as the debates on slavery at the beginning of the Republic and as new as present-day controversies concerning laws and court decisions concerning abortion. Widely different perspectives on the general problem are contained in thirteen essays in *The Moral Foundations of the American Republic*, edited by Robert H. Horwitz.

The relationship between constitutional law and the Constitution is a problem that is somewhat more technical in character than that between moral principles and the Constitution. There is a vast literature on the topic. Henry Abraham's *The Judiciary: The Supreme Court in the Governmental Process* sets forth a reasoned overview. Three critical studies of the way in which the dominant present-day view of the relationship came into being—a view epitomized in Justice Brennan's 1985 speech and in Laurence Tribe's textbook—are particularly worth noting: Christopher Wolfe's *The Rise of Modern Judicial Review*; Gary L. McDowell's *Equity and the Constitution;* and Matthew Franck's *Against the Imperial Judiciary.*

CONTINUOUS FOUNDING

At a bicentennial celebration of the Northwest Ordinance, in 1887, in Marietta, Ohio, Senator George Hoar of Massachusetts spoke of the effects of that Organic Law on the course of constitutional development in America. He said: "The Ordinance belongs with the Declaration of Independence and the Constitution. It is one of the three title-deeds of American constitutional liberty."[50] Peter S. Onuf, who cites this statement as a typical appraisal of the linkage of freedom in the Northwest Territory to the founding of the Republic, and who notes, repeatedly, the attribution of the authorship of the Ordinance to Thomas Jefferson, sums it up thus: ". . . if the principles of freedom could be traced back to Jefferson and the founders, it was the 'free men' of the northwestern states who kept them alive. It was this sense of participating in a continuous founding—a vast cooperative enterprise linking contemporary northwesterners to the American Founding Fathers—that most inspired publicists."[51]

Onuf's phrase, "continuous founding," is a felicitous one. I suggest that it is as applicable to us, today, as "free men" of the end of the twentieth century, as it was to the "free men" of the nineteenth century, in the old Northwest. For we may be said to engage, in our souls, in a "continuous founding" as we rethink what the Organic Laws mean; and we do so even more if and when we permit the principles that inform them to shape what we say and do in our conduct toward the American constitutional order. In so thinking, speaking, and acting, we may come to grasp what Justice William Johnson, of South Carolina, meant when he said: "In the Constitution of the United States—the most wonderful instrument ever drawn by the hand of man—there is a comprehension and precision that is unparalleled; and I can truly say that after spending my life studying it, I still find in it some new excellence."[52]

---

50. Onuf, *Statehood and Union,* p. 133.
51. Ibid., p. 147.
52. In *Elkinson* v. *Deliesseline,* 8 Federal Cases 593 (1823).

THE ORGANIC LAWS
OF
THE UNITED STATES
OF AMERICA

THE DECLARATION
OF INDEPENDENCE (1776)[1]

IN CONGRESS, JULY 4, 1776.
THE UNANIMOUS DECLARATION OF THE THIRTEEN UNITED STATES OF AMERICA.

When in the Course of human Events, it becomes necessary for one People to dissolve the Political Bands which have connected them

---

1. The delegates of the United Colonies of New Hampshire; Massachusetts Bay; Rhode Island and Providence Plantations; Connecticut; New York; New Jersey; Pennsylvania; New Castle, Kent, and Sussex, in Delaware; Maryland; Virginia; North Carolina, and South Carolina, In Congress assembled at Philadelphia, *Resolved* on the 10th of May, 1776, to recommend to the respective assemblies and conventions of the United Colonies, where no government sufficient to the exigencies of their affairs had been established, to adopt such a government as should, in the opinion of the representatives of the people, best conduce to the happiness and safety of their constituents in particular, and of America in general. A preamble to this resolution, agreed to on the 15th of May, stated the intention to be totally to suppress the exercise of every kind of authority under the British crown. On the 7th of June, certain resolutions respecting independency were moved and seconded. On the 10th of June it was

with another, and to assume among the Powers of the Earth, the separate and equal Station to which the Laws of Nature and of

---

resolved, that a committee should be appointed to prepare a declaration to the following effect:

"That the United Colonies are, and of right ought to be, free and Independent States; that they are absolved from all allegiance to the British crown; and that all political connection between them and the State of Great Britain is, and ought to be, totally dissolved." On the preceding day it was determined that the committee for preparing the declaration should consist of five, and they were chosen accordingly, in the following order: Mr. Jefferson, Mr. J. Adams, Mr. Franklin, Mr. Sherman, Mr. R. R. Livingston. On the 11th of June a resolution was passed to appoint a committee to prepare and digest the form of a confederation to be entered into between the colonies, and another committee to prepare a plan of treaties to be proposed to foreign powers. On the 12th of June, it was resolved, that a committee of Congress should be appointed by the name of a board of war and ordnance, to consist of five members. On the 25th of June, a declaration of the deputies of Pennsylvania, met in provincial conference, expressing their willingness to concur in a vote declaring the United Colonies free and independent States, was laid before Congress and read. On the 28th of June, the committee appointed to prepare a declaration of independence brought in a draught, which was read, and ordered to lie on the table. On the 1st of July, a resolution of the convention of Maryland, passed the 28th of June, authorizing the deputies of that colony to concur in declaring the United Colonies free and independent States, was laid before Congress and read. On the same day Congress resolved itself into a committee of the whole, to take into consideration the resolution respecting independency. On the 2d of July, a resolution declaring the colonies free and independent States, was adopted. A declaration to that effect was, on the same and the following days, taken into further consideration. Finally, on the 4th of July, the Declaration of Independence was agreed to, engrossed on paper, signed by John Hancock as president, and directed to be sent to the several assemblies, conventions, and committees, or councils of safety, and to the several commanding officers of the continental troops, and to be proclaimed in each of the United States, and at the head of the Army. It was also ordered to be entered upon the Journals of Congress, and on the 2d of August, a copy engrossed on parchment was signed by all but one of the fifty-six signers whose names are appended to it. That one was Matthew Thornton, of New Hampshire, who on taking his seat in November asked and obtained the privilege of signing it. Several who signed it on the 2d of August were absent when it was adopted on the 4th of July, but, approving of it, they thus signified their approbation.

Note.—The proof of this document, as published above, was read by Mr. Ferdinand Jefferson, the Keeper of the Rolls at the Department of State, at Washington, who compared it with the fac-simile of the original in his custody. He says:

Nature's God entitle them, a decent Respect to the Opinions of Mankind requires that they should declare the causes which impel them to the Separation.

We hold these Truths to be self-evident, that all Men are created equal, that they are endowed by their Creator with certain unalienable Rights, that among these are Life, Liberty, and the Pursuit of Happiness—That to secure these Rights, Governments are instituted among Men, deriving their just Powers from the Consent of the Governed, that whenever any Form of Government becomes destructive of these Ends, it is the Right of the People to alter or to abolish it, and to institute new Government, laying its Foundation on such Principles, and organizing its Powers in such Form, as to them shall seem most likely to effect their Safety and Happiness. Prudence, indeed, will dictate that Governments long established should not be changed for light and transient Causes; and accordingly all Experience hath shewn, that Mankind are more disposed to suffer, while Evils are sufferable, than to right themselves by abolishing the Forms to which they are accustomed. But when a long Train of Abuses and Usurpations, pursuing invariably the same Object, evinces a Design to reduce them under absolute Despotism, it is their Right, it is their Duty, to throw off such Government, and to provide new Guards for their future Security. Such has been the patient Sufferance of these Colonies; and such is now the Necessity which constrains them to alter their former Systems of Government. The History of the present King of Great-Britain is a History of repeated Injuries and Usurpations, all having in direct Object the Establishment of an absolute Tyranny over these States. To prove this, let Facts be submitted to a candid World:

"In the fac-simile, as in the original, the whole instrument runs on without a break, but dashes are mostly inserted. I have, in this copy, followed the arrangement of paragraphs adopted in the publication of the Declaration in the newspaper of John Dunlap, and as printed by him for the Congress, which printed copy is inserted in the original Journal of the old Congress. The same paragraphs are also made by the author, in the original draught preserved in the Department of State."

He has refused his Assent to Laws, the most wholesome and necessary for the public Good.

He has forbidden his Governors to pass Laws of immediate and pressing Importance, unless suspended in their Operation till his Assent should be obtained; and when so suspended, he has utterly neglected to attend to them.

He has refused to pass other Laws for the Accommodation of large Districts of People, unless those People would relinquish the Right of Representation in the Legislature, a Right inestimable to them, and formidable to Tyrants only.

He has called together Legislative Bodies at Places unusual, uncomfortable, and distant from the Depository of their public Records, for the sole Purpose of fatiguing them into Compliance with his Measures.

He has dissolved Representative Houses repeatedly, for opposing with manly Firmness his Invasions on the Rights of the People.

He has refused for a long Time, after such Dissolutions, to cause others to be elected; whereby the Legislative Powers, incapable of Annihilation, have returned to the People at large for their exercise; the State remaining in the mean time exposed to all the Dangers of Invasion from without, and Convulsions within.

He has endeavoured to prevent the Population of these States; for that Purpose obstructing the Laws for Naturalization of Foreigners; refusing to pass others to encourage their Migrations hither, and raising the Conditions of new Appropriations of Lands.

He has obstructed the Administration of Justice, by refusing his Assent to Laws for establishing Judiciary Powers.

He has made Judges dependent on his Will alone, for the Tenure of their Offices, and the Amount and Payment of their Salaries.

He has erected a Multitude of new Offices, and sent hither Swarms of Officers to harass our People, and eat out their Substance.

He has kept among us, in Times of Peace, Standing Armies, without the consent of our Legislatures.

He has affected to render the Military independent of and superior to the Civil Power.

He has combined with others to subject us to a Jurisdiction foreign to our Constitution, and unacknowledged by our Laws; giving his Assent to their Acts of pretended Legislation:

For quartering large Bodies of Armed Troops among us:

For protecting them, by a mock Trial, from Punishment for any Murders which they should commit on the Inhabitants of these States:

For cutting off our Trade with all Parts of the World:

For imposing Taxes on us without our Consent:

For depriving us, in many Cases, of the Benefits of Trial by Jury:

For transporting us beyond Seas to be tried for pretended Offences:

For abolishing the free System of English Laws in a neighbouring Province, establishing therein an arbitrary Government, and enlarging its Boundaries, so as to render it at once an Example and fit Instrument for introducing the same absolute Rule into these Colonies:

For taking away our Charters, abolishing our most valuable Laws, and altering fundamentally the Forms of our Governments:

For suspending our own Legislatures, and declaring themselves invested with Power to legislate for us in all Cases whatsoever.

He has abdicated Government here, by declaring us out of his Protection and waging War against us.

He has plundered our Seas, ravaged our Coasts, burnt our Towns, and destroyed the Lives of our People.

He is, at this Time, transporting large Armies of foreign Mercenaries to compleat the Works of Death, Desolation, and Tyranny, already begun with circumstances of Cruelty and Perfidy, scarcely paralleled in the most barbarous Ages, and totally unworthy the Head of a civilized Nation.

He has constrained our fellow Citizens taken Captive on the

high Seas to bear Arms against their Country, to become the Executioners of their Friends and Brethren, or to fall themselves by their Hands.

He has excited domestic Insurrections amongst us, and has endeavoured to bring on the Inhabitants of our Frontiers, the merciless Indian Savages, whose known Rule of Warfare, is an undistinguished Destruction, of all Ages, Sexes and Conditions.

In every stage of these Oppressions we have Petitioned for Redress in the most humble Terms: Our repeated Petitions have been answered only by repeated Injury. A Prince, whose Character is thus marked by every act which may define a Tyrant, is unfit to be the Ruler of a free People.

Nor have we been wanting in Attentions to our British Brethren. We have warned them from Time to Time of Attempts by their Legislature to extend an unwarrantable Jurisdiction over us. We have reminded them of the Circumstances of our Emigration and Settlement here. We have appealed to their native Justice and Magnanimity, and we have conjured them by the Ties of our common Kindred to disavow these Usurpations, which, would inevitably interrupt our Connections and Correspondence. They too have been deaf to the Voice of Justice and of Consanguinity. We must, therefore, acquiesce in the Necessity, which denounces our Separation, and hold them, as we hold the rest of Mankind, Enemies in War, in Peace, Friends.

We, therefore, the Representatives of the UNITED STATES OF AMERICA, in General Congress, Assembled, appealing to the Supreme Judge of the World for the Rectitude of our Intentions, do, in the Name, and by Authority of the good People of these Colonies, solemnly Publish and Declare, That these United Colonies are, and of Right ought to be, Free and Independent States; that they are absolved from all Allegiance to the British Crown, and that all political Connection between them and the State of Great-Britain, is and ought to be totally dissolved; and that as Free and Independent States, they have full Power to levy War, conclude Peace, contract Alliances, establish Commerce, and to do all other Acts and Things which Independent States may of right do. And for the support of this Declaration, with a firm Reliance on the Protection of divine Providence, we mutually pledge to each other our Lives, our Fortunes, and our sacred Honor.

JOHN HANCOCK

New Hampshire

JOSIAH BARTLETT,   MATTHEW THORNTON.
WM WHIPPLE,

Massachusetts Bay

SAML. ADAMS,   ROBT. TREAT PAINE,
JOHN ADAMS,   ELBRIDGE GERRY.

Rhode Island

STEP. HOPKINS,   WILLIAM ELLERY.

Connecticut

ROGER SHERMAN,   WM. WILLIAMS,
SAM'EL HUNTINGTON,   OLIVER WOLCOTT.

New York

WM. FLOYD,   FRANS. LEWIS,
PHIL. LIVINGSTON,   LEWIS MORRIS.

New Jersey

RICHD. STOCKTON,   JOHN HART,
JNO. WITHERSPOON,   ABRA. CLARK.
FRAS. HOPKINSON,

Pennsylvania

ROBT. MORRIS,
BENJAMIN RUSH,
BENJA. FRANKLIN,
JOHN MORTON,
GEO. CLYMER,

JAS. SMITH,
GEO. TAYLOR,
JAMES WILSON,
GEO. ROSS.

Delaware

CAESAR RODNEY,
GEO. READ,

THO M'KEAN.

Maryland

SAMUEL CHASE,
WM. PACA,
THOS. STONE,

CHARLES CARROLL, OF
CARROLLTON.

Virginia

GEORGE WYTHE,
RICHARD HENRY LEE,
THS. JEFFERSON,
BENJA. HARRISON,

THOS. NELSON, JR.
FRANCIS LIGHTFOOT LEE,
CARTER BRAXTON.

North Carolina

WM. HOOPER,
JOSEPH HEWES,

JOHN PENN.

South Carolina

THOS. HEYWARD, JUNR.
EDWARD RUTLEDGE,

THOMAS LYNCH, JUNR.
ARTHUR MIDDLETON.

Georgia

BUTTON GWINNETT,   GEO. WALTON.[2]
LYMAN HALL,

---

2. Note.—Mr. Ferdinand Jefferson, Keeper of the Rolls in the Department of State, at Washington, says: "The names of the signers are spelt above as in the fac-simile of the original, but the punctuation of them is not always the same; neither do the names of the States appear in the fac-simile of the original. The names of the signers of each State are grouped together in the fac-simile of the original, except the name of Matthew Thornton, which follows that of Oliver Wolcott."

ARTICLES OF CONFEDERATION (1777)[3]

To all to whom these Presents shall come, we the under signed Delegates of the States affixed to our Names, send greeting.

---

3. Congress *Resolved,* on the 11th of June, 1776, that a committee should be appointed to prepare and digest the form of a confederation to be entered into between the Colonies; and on the day following, after it had been determined that the committee should consist of a member from each Colony, the following persons were appointed to perform that duty, to wit: Mr. Bartlett, Mr. S. Adams, Mr. Hopkins, Mr. Sherman, Mr. R. R. Livingston, Mr. Dickinson, Mr. M'Kean, Mr. Stone, Mr. Nelson, Mr. Hewes, Mr. E. Rutledge, and Mr. Gwinnett. Upon the report of this committee, the subject was, from time to time, debated, until the 15th of November, 1777, when a copy of the confederation being made out, and sundry amendments made in the diction, without altering the sense, the same was finally agreed to. Congress, at the same time, directed that the articles should be proposed to the legislatures of all the United States, to be considered, and if approved of by them, they were advised to authorize their delegates to ratify the same in the Congress of the United States; which being done, the same should become conclusive. Three hundred copies of the Articles of Confederation were ordered to be printed for the use of Congress; and on the 17th of November, the form of a circular letter to accompany them was brought in by a committee appointed to prepare it, and being agreed to, thirteen copies of it were ordered to

Whereas the Delegates of the United States of America, in Congress assembled, did, on the 15th day of November, in the Year of Our Lord One thousand Seven Hundred and Seventy seven, and in the Second Year of the Independence of America, agree to certain articles of Confederation and perpetual Union between the States of Newhampshire, Massachusetts-bay, Rhodeisland and Providence Plantations, Connecticut, New York, New Jersey, Pennsylvania,

---

be made out, to be signed by the president and forwarded to the several States, with copies of the confederation. On the 29th of November ensuing, a committee of three was appointed, to procure a translation of the articles to be made into the French language, and to report an address to the inhabitants of Canada, &c. On the 26th of June, 1778, the form of a ratification of the Articles of Confederation was adopted, and, it having been engrossed on parchment, it was signed on the 9th of July on the part and in behalf of their respective States, by the delegates of New Hampshire, Massachusetts Bay, Rhode Island and Providence Plantations, Connecticut, New York, Pennsylvania, Virginia, and South Carolina, agreeably to the powers vested in them. The delegates of North Carolina signed on the 21st of July, those of Georgia on the 24th of July, and those of New Jersey on the 26th of November following. On the 5th of May, 1779, Mr. Dickinson and Mr. Van Dyke signed in behalf of the State of Delaware, Mr. M'Kean having previously signed in February, at which time he produced a power to that effect. Maryland did not ratify until the year 1781. She had instructed her delegates, on the 15th of December, 1778, not to agree to the confederation until matters respecting the western lands should be settled on principles of equity and sound policy; but, on the 30th of January, 1781, finding that the enemies of the country took advantage of the circumstance to disseminate opinions of an ultimate dissolution of the Union, the legislature of the State passed an act to empower their delegates to subscribe and ratify the articles, which was accordingly done by Mr. Hanson and Mr. Carroll, on the 1st of March of that year, which completed the ratifications of the act; and Congress assembled on the 2d of March under the new powers.

Note.—The proof of this document, as published above, was read by Mr. Ferdinand Jefferson, the Keeper of the Rolls of the Department of State. at Washington, who compared it with the original in his custody. He says: "The initial letters of many of the words in the original of this instrument are capitals, but as no system appears to have been observed, the same words sometimes beginning with a capital and sometimes with a small letter, I have thought it best not to undertake to follow the original in this particular. Moreover, there are three forms of the letter s: the capital S, the small s and the long s, the last being used indiscriminately to words that should begin with a capital and those that should begin with a small s."

Delaware, Maryland, Virginia, North-Carolina, South-Carolina, and Georgia in the words following, viz. *"Articles of Confederation and perpetual Union between the states of Newhampshire, Massachusetts-bay, Rhodeisland and Providence Plantations, Connecticut, New-York, New-Jersey, Pennsylvania, Delaware, Maryland, Virginia, North-Carolina, South-Carolina and Georgia.*

Article I. The Stile of this confederacy shall be "The United States of America."

Article II. Each state retains its sovereignty, freedom, and independence, and every Power, Jurisdiction and right, which is not by this confederation expressly delegated to the United States, in Congress assembled.

Article III. The said states hereby severally enter into a firm league of friendship with each other, for their common defence, the security of their Liberties, and their mutual and general welfare, binding themselves to assist each other, against all force offered to, or attacks made upon them, or any of them, on account of religion, sovereignty, trade, or any other pretence whatever.

Article IV. The better to secure and perpetuate mutual friendship and intercourse among the people of the different states in this union, the free inhabitants of each of these states, paupers, vagabonds and fugitives from justice excepted, shall be entitled to all privileges and immunities of free citizens in the several states; and the people of each state shall have free ingress and regress to and from any other state, and shall enjoy therein all the privileges of trade and commerce, subject to the same duties, impositions and restrictions as the inhabitants thereof respectively, provided that such restriction shall not extend so far as to prevent the removal of property imported into any state, to any other state, of which the Owner is an inhabitant; provided also that no imposition, duties or restriction shall be laid by any state, on the property of the united states, or either of them.

If any Person guilty of, or charged with treason, felony, or other high misdemeanor in any state, shall flee from Justice, and be found in any of the united states, he shall, upon demand of the Governor or executive power, of the state from which he fled, be delivered up and removed to the state having jurisdiction of his offence.

Full faith and credit shall be given in each of these states to the records, acts and judicial proceedings of the courts and magistrates of every other state.

Article V. For the more convenient management of the general interests of the united states, delegates shall be annually appointed in such manner as the legislature of each state shall direct, to meet in Congress on the first Monday in November, in every year, with a power reserved to each state, to recal [*sic*] its delegates, or any of them, at any time within the year, and to send others in their stead, for the remainder of the Year.

No state shall be represented in Congress by less than two, nor by more than seven Members; and no person shall be capable of being a delegate for more than three years in any term of six years; nor shall any person, being a delegate, be capable of holding any office under the united states, for which he, or another for his benefit receives any salary, fees or emolument of any kind.

Each state shall maintain its own delegates in a meeting of the states, and while they act as members of the committee of the states.

In determining questions in the united states in Congress assembled, each state shall have one vote.

Freedom of speech and debate in Congress shall not be impeached or questioned in any Court, or place out of Congress, and the members of congress shall be protected in their persons from arrests and imprisonments, during the time of their going to and from, and attendance on congress, except for treason, felony, or breach of the peace.

Article VI. No state, without the Consent of the united states in congress assembled, shall send any embassy to, or receive any embassy from, or enter into any conference, agreement, alliance or treaty with any King prince or state; nor shall any person holding any office of profit or trust under the united states, or any of them, accept of any present, emolument, office or title of any kind whatever from any king, prince or foreign state; nor shall the united states in congress assembled, or any of them, grant any title of nobility.

No two or more states shall enter into any treaty, confederation or alliance whatever between them, without the consent of the united states in congress assembled, specifying accurately the purposes for which the same is to be entered into, and how long it shall continue.

No state shall lay any imposts or duties, which may interfere with any stipulations in treaties, entered into by the united states in congress assembled, with any king, prince or state, in pursuance of any treaties already proposed by congress, to the courts of France and Spain.

No vessels of war shall be kept up in time of peace by any state, except such number only, as shall be deemed necessary by the united states in congress assembled, for the defence of such state, or its trade; nor shall any body of forces be kept up by any state, in time of peace, except such number only, as in the judgment of the united states, in congress assembled, shall be deemed requisite to garrison the forts necessary for the defence of such state; but every state shall always keep up a well regulated and disciplined militia, sufficiently armed and accoutred, and shall provide and constantly have ready for use, in public stores, a due number of field pieces and tents, and a proper quantity of arms, ammunition and camp equipage.

No state shall engage in any war without the consent of the united states in congress assembled, unless such state be actually invaded by enemies, or shall have received certain advice of a resolution being formed by some nation of Indians to invade such state, and the danger is so imminent as not to admit of a delay till the united states in congress assembled can be consulted: nor shall any state grant commissions to any ships or vessels of war, nor letters of marque or reprisal, except it be after a declaration of war by the united states in congress assembled, and then only against the kingdom or state and the subjects thereof, against which war has been so declared, and under such regulations as shall be established by the united states in congress assembled, unless such state be infested by pirates, in which case vessels of war may be fitted out for that occasion, and kept so long as the danger shall continue, or until the united states in congress assembled, shall determine otherwise.

Article VII. When land-forces are raised by any state for the common defence, all officers of or under the rank of colonel, shall be appointed by the legislature of each state respectively, by whom such forces shall be raised, or in such manner as such state shall direct, and all vacancies shall be filled up by the State which first made the appointment.

Article VIII. All charges of war, and all other expences that shall be incurred for the common defence or general welfare, and allowed by the united states in congress assembled, shall be defrayed out of a common treasury, which shall be supplied by the several states in proportion to the value of all land within each state, granted to or surveyed for any Person, as such land and the buildings and improvements thereon shall be estimated according to such mode as the united states in congress assembled, shall from time to time direct and appoint.

The taxes for paying that proportion shall be laid and levied by the authority and direction of the legislatures of the several states within the time agreed upon by the united states in congress assembled.

Article IX. The united states in congress assembled, shall have the sole and exclusive right and power of determining on peace and war, except in the cases mentioned in the sixth article—of sending and receiving ambassadors—entering into treaties and alliances, provided that no treaty of commerce shall be made whereby the legislative power of the respective states shall be restrained from imposing such imposts and duties on foreigners as their own people are subjected to, or from prohibiting the exportation or importation of any species of goods or commodities, whatsoever—of establishing rules for deciding in all cases, what captures on land or water shall be legal, and in what manner prizes taken by land or naval forces in the service of the united states shall be divided or appropriated—of granting letters of marque and reprisal in times of peace—appointing courts for the trial of piracies and felonies committed on the high seas and establishing courts for receiving and determining finally appeals in all cases of captures, provided that no member of congress shall be appointed a judge of any of the said courts.

The united states in congress assembled shall also be the last resort on appeal in all disputes and differences now subsisting or that hereafter may arise between two or more states concerning boundary, jurisdiction or any other cause whatever; which authority shall always be exercised in the manner following. Whenever the legislative or executive authority or lawful agent of any state in controversy with another shall present a petition to congress stating the matter in question and praying for a hearing, notice thereof shall be given by order of congress to the legislative or executive authority of the other state in controversy, and a day assigned for the appearance of the parties by their lawful agents, who shall then be directed to appoint by joint consent, commissioners or judges to constitute a court for hearing and determining the matter in question: but if they cannot agree, congress shall name three persons out of each of the united states, and from the list of such persons each party shall alternately strike out one, the petitioners beginning, until the number shall be reduced to thirteen; and from that number not less than seven, nor more than nine names as congress shall direct, shall in the presence of congress be drawn out by lot, and the persons whose names shall be so drawn or any five of them, shall be commissioners or judges, to hear and finally determine the controversy, so always as a major part of the judges who shall hear the cause shall agree in the determination: and if either party shall neglect to attend at the day appointed, without showing reasons, which congress shall judge sufficient, or being present shall refuse to strike, the congress shall proceed to nominate three persons out of each state, and the secretary of congress shall strike in behalf of such party absent or refusing; and the judgment and sentence of the court to be appointed, in the manner before prescribed, shall be final and conclusive; and if any of the parties shall refuse to submit to the authority of such court, or to appear or defend their claim or cause, the court shall nevertheless proceed to pronounce sentence, or judgment, which shall in like manner be final and decisive, the judgment or sentence and other proceedings being in either case transmitted to congress, and lodged among the acts of congress for the security of the parties concerned: provided that every commissioner, before he sits in judgment, shall take an oath to be administered by one of the judges of the supreme or superior court of the state, where the cause shall be tried, "well and truly to hear and determine the matter in question, according to the best of his judgment, without favour, affection or hope of reward:" provided also, that no state shall be deprived of territory for the benefit of the united states.

All controversies concerning the private right of soil claimed under different grants of two or more states, whose jurisdictions as they may respect such lands, and the states which passed such grants are adjusted, the said grants or either of them being at the same time claimed to have originated antecedent to such settlement of jurisdiction, shall on the petition of either party to the congress of the united states, be finally determined as near as may be in the same manner as is before prescribed for deciding disputes respecting territorial jurisdiction between different states.

The united states in congress assembled shall also have the sole and exclusive right and power of regulating the alloy and value of coin struck by their own authority, or by that of the respective states—fixing the standard of weights and measures throughout the united states—regulating the trade and managing all affairs with the Indians, not members of any of the states, provided that the legislative right of any state within its own limits be not infringed or violated—establishing or regulating post-offices from one state to another, throughout all the united states, and exacting such postage on the papers passing thro' the same as may be requisite to defray the expences of the said office—appointing all officers of the land forces, in the service of the united states, excepting regimental officers—appointing all the officers of the naval forces, and commissioning all officers whatever in the service of the united states—making rules for the government and regulation of the said land and naval forces, and directing their operations.

The united states in congress assembled shall have authority to appoint a committee, to sit in the recess of congress, to be denominated "A Committee of the States," and to consist of one delegate from each state; and to appoint such other committees and civil officers as may be necessary for managing the general affairs of the united states under their direction—to appoint one of their number to preside, provided that no person be allowed to serve in the office of president more than one year in any term of three years; to ascertain the necessary sums of money to be raised for the service of the united states, and to appropriate and apply the same for defraying the public expences—to borrow money, or emit bills on the credit of the united states, transmitting every half year to the respective states an account of the sums of money so borrowed or emitted, — to build and equip a navy—to agree upon the number of land forces, and to make requisitions from each state for its quota, in proportion to the number of white inhabitants in such state; which requisition shall be binding, and thereupon the legislature of each state shall appoint the regimental officers, raise the men and cloath [sic], arm and equip them in a soldier like manner, at the expence of the united states; and the officers and men so cloathed, armed and equipped shall march to the place appointed, and within the time agreed on by the united states in congress assembled: But if the united states in congress assembled shall, on consideration of circumstances judge proper that any state should not raise men, or should raise a smaller number than its quota, and that any other state should raise a greater number of men than the quota thereof, such extra number shall be raised, officered, cloathed, armed and equipped in the same manner as the quota of such state, unless the legislature of such state shall judge that such extra number cannot be safely spared out of the same, in which case they shall raise, officer, cloath, arm and equip as many of such extra number as they judge can be safely spared. And the officers and men so cloathed, armed and equipped, shall march to the place appointed, and within the time agreed on by the united states in congress assembled.

The united states in congress assembled shall never engage in a war, nor grant letters of marque and reprisal in time of peace, nor enter into any treaties or alliances, nor coin money, nor regulate the value thereof, nor ascertain the sums and expences necessary for the defence and welfare of the united states, or any of them, nor emit bills, nor borrow money on the credit of the united states, nor appropriate money, nor agree upon the number of vessels of war, to be built or purchased, or the number of land or sea forces to be raised, nor appoint a commander in chief of the army or navy, unless nine states assent to the same: nor shall a question on any other point, except for adjourning from day to day be determined, unless by the votes of a majority of the united states in congress assembled.

The congress of the united states shall have power to adjourn to any time within the year, and to any place within the united states, so that no period of adjournment be for a longer duration than the space of six Months, and shall publish the Journal of their proceedings monthly, except such parts thereof relating to treaties, alliances or military operations, as in their judgment require secrecy; and the yeas and nays of the delegates of each state on any question shall be entered on the Journal, when it is desired by any delegate; and the delegates of a state, or any of them, at his or their request shall be furnished with a transcript of the said Journal, except such parts as are above excepted, to lay before the legislatures of the several states.

Article X. The committee of the states, or any nine of them, shall be authorized to execute, in the recess of congress, such of the powers of congress as the united states in congress assembled, by the consent of nine states, shall from time to time think expedient to vest them with; provided that no power be delegated to the said committee, for the exercise of which, by the articles of confederation, the voice of nine states in the congress of the united states assembled is requisite.

Article XI. Canada acceding to this confederation, and joining in the measures of the united states, shall be admitted into, and entitled to all the advantages of this union: but no other colony shall be admitted into the same, unless such admission be agreed to by nine states.

Article XII. All bills of credit emitted, monies borrowed and debts contracted by, or under the authority of congress, before the assembling of the united states, in pursuance of the present confederation, shall be deemed and considered as a charge against the united states, for payment and satisfaction whereof the said united states, and the public faith are hereby solemnly pledged.

Article XIII. Every state shall abide by the determinations of the united states in congress assembled, on all questions which by this confederation are submitted to them. And the Articles of this confederation shall be inviolably observed by every state, and the union shall be perpetual; nor shall any alteration at any time hereafter be made in any of them; unless such alteration be agreed to in a congress of the united states, and be afterwards confirmed by the legislatures of every state.

And Whereas it hath pleased the Great Governor of the World to incline the hearts of the legislatures we respectively represent in congress, to approve of, and to authorize us to ratify the said articles of confederation and perpetual union, Know Ye that we the undersigned delegates, by virtue of the power and authority to us given for that purpose, do by these presents, in the name and in behalf of our respective constituents, fully and entirely ratify and confirm each and every of the said articles of confederation and perpetual union, and all and singular the matters and things therein contained: And we do further solemnly plight and engage the faith of our respective constituents, that they shall abide by the determinations of the united states in congress assembled, on all questions, which by the said confederation are submitted to them. And that the articles thereof shall be inviolably observed by the states we respectively represent, and that the union shall be perpetual. In Witness whereof we have hereunto set our hands in Congress. Done at Philadelphia in the state of Pennsylvania the ninth day of July, in the Year of our Lord one Thousand seven Hundred and Seventy-eight, and in the third year of the independence of America.[4]

On the part & behalf of the State of New Hampshire

Josiah BARTLETT,

JOHN WENTWORTH, JUNR
August 8th, 1778.

On the part and behalf of the State of Massachusetts Bay

JOHN HANCOCK,
SAMUEL ADAMS,
ELBRIDGE GERRY,

FRANCIS DANA,
JAMES LOVELL,
SAMUEL HOLTEN.

On the part and behalf of the
State of Rhode-Island and Providence Plantations

WILLIAM ELLERY,
HENRY MARCHANT,

JOHN COLLINS.

On the part and behalf of the State of Connecticut

ROGER SHERMAN,
SAMUEL HUNTINGTON,
OLIVER WOLCOTT,

TITUS HOSMER,
ANDREW ADAMS.

On the part and behalf of the State of New York

JAS DUANE,
FRA. LEWIS,

WM. DUER,
GOUV. MORRIS.

---

4. From the circumstances of delegates from the same State having signed the Articles of Confederation at different times, as appears by the dates, it is probable they affixed their names as they happened to be present in Congress, after they had been authorized by their constituents.

On the Part and in Behalf of the State of New Jersey,
Novr. 26th, 1778

Jno Witherspoon,   Nathl. Scudder.

On the part and behalf of the State of Pennsylvania

Robt. Morris,   William Clingan,
Daniel Roberdeau,   Joseph Reed, 22d July, 1778.
Jona. Bayard Smith,

On the part & behalf of the State of Delaware

Tho. M'Kean, Feby. 12, 1779, Nicholas Van Dyke.
John Dickinson,
 May 5th, 1779,

On the part and behalf of the State of Maryland

John Hanson, March 1, 1781, Daniel Carroll, Mar. 1, 1781.

On the Part and Behalf of the State of Virginia

Richard Henry Lee,   Jno. Harvie,
John Banister,   Francis Lightfoot Lee.
Thomas Adams,

On the part and behalf of the State of No. Carolina

John Penn, July 21st, 1778, Corns. Harnett,
           Jno. Williams.

On the part & behalf of the State of South Carolina

Henry Laurens,   Richd. Hutson,
William Henry Drayton,   Thos. Heyward, junr.
Jno. Mathews,

On the part & behalf of the State of Georgia

Jno. Walton, 24th July, 1778, Edwd. Telfair,
           Edwd. Langworthy.

ORDINANCE OF 1787: THE NORTHWEST TERRITORIAL GOVERNMENT

[THE CONFEDERATE CONGRESS, JULY 13, 1787]

AN ORDINANCE FOR THE GOVERNMENT OF THE TERRITORY OF THE UNITED STATES, NORTH-WEST OF THE RIVER OHIO

[Section 1.] *BE IT ORDAINED by the United States in Congress assembled,* That the said territory, for the purposes of temporary government, be one district; subject, however, to be divided into two districts, as future circumstances may, in the opinion of Congress, make it expedient.

[Section 2.] *Be it ordained by the authority aforesaid,* That the estates both of resident and non-resident proprietors in the said territory, dying intestate, shall descend to, and be distributed among their children, and the descendants of a deceased child in equal parts; the descendants of a deceased child or grand-child, to take the share of their deceased parent in equal parts among them: And where there shall be no children or descendants, then in equal parts

97

to the next of kin, in equal degree; and among collaterals, the children of a deceased brother or sister of the intestate, shall have in equal parts among them their deceased parents share; and there shall in no case be a distinction between kindred of the whole and half blood; saving in all cases to the widow of the intestate, her third part of the real estate for life, and one third part of the personal estate; and this law relative to descents and dower, shall remain in full force until altered by the legislature of the district ——— And until the governor and judges shall adopt laws as herein after mentioned, estates in the said territory may be devised or bequeathed by wills in writing, signed and sealed by him or her, in whom the estate may be, (being of full age) and attested by three witnesses;—and real estates may be conveyed by lease and release, or bargain and sale, signed, sealed, and delivered by the person being of full age, in whom the estate may be, and attested by two witnesses, provided such wills be duly proved, and such conveyances be acknowledged, or the execution thereof duly proved, and be recorded within one year after proper magistrates, courts, and registers shall be appointed for that purpose; and personal property may be transferred by delivery, saving, however, to the French and Canadian inhabitants, and other settlers of the Kaskaskies, Saint Vincent's, and the neighbouring villages, who have heretofore professed themselves citizens of Virginia, their laws and customs now in force among them, relative to the descent and conveyance of property.

[Section 3.] *Be it ordained by the authority aforesaid,* That there shall be appointed from time to time, by Congress, a governor, whose commission shall continue in force for the term of three years, unless sooner revoked by Congress; he shall reside in the district, and have a freehold estate therein, in one thousand acres of land, while in the exercise of his office.

[Section 4.] There shall be appointed from time to time, by Congress, a secretary, whose commission shall continue in force for four years, unless sooner revoked, he shall reside in the district, and have a freehold estate therein, in five hundred acres of land, while in the exercise of his office; it shall be his duty to keep and preserve the acts and laws passed by the legislature, and the public records of the district, and the proceedings of the governor in his executive department; and transmit authentic copies of such acts and proceedings, every six months, to the secretary of Congress: There shall also be appointed a court to consist of three judges, any two of whom to form a court, who shall have a common law juris-diction, and reside in the district, and have each therein a freehold estate in five hundred acres of land, while in the exercise of their offices; and their commissions shall continue in force during good behaviour.

[Section 5.] The governor and judges, or a majority of them, shall adopt and publish in the district, such laws of the original states, criminal and civil, as may be necessary, and best suited to the circumstances of the district, and report them to Congress, from time to time, which laws shall be in force in the district until the organization of the general assembly therein, unless disapproved of by Congress; but afterwards the legislature shall have authority to alter them as they shall think fit.

[Section 6.] The governor for the time being, shall be com-mander in chief of the militia, appoint and commission all officers in the same, below the rank of general officers; all general officers shall be appointed and commissioned by Congress.

[Section 7.] Previous to the organization of the general as-sembly, the governor shall appoint such magistrates and other civil officers, in each county or township, as he shall find necessary for the preservation of the peace and good order in the same: After the general assembly shall be organized, the powers and duties of mag-istrates and other civil officers shall be regulated and defined by the said assembly; but all magistrates and other civil officers, not herein otherwise directed, shall, during the continuance of this tem-porary government, be appointed by the governor.

[Section 8.] For the prevention of crimes and injuries, the laws to be adopted or made shall have force in all parts of the district, and for the execution of process, criminal and civil, the governor shall make proper divisions thereof—and he shall proceed from time to time, as circumstances may require, to lay out the parts of the district in which the Indian titles shall have been extinguished, into counties and townships, subject, however, to such alterations as may thereafter be made by the legislature.

[Section 9.] So soon as there shall be five thousand free male inhabitants, of full age, in the district, upon giving proof thereof to the governor, they shall receive authority, with time and place, to elect representatives from their counties or townships, to represent them in the general assembly; *provided* that for every five hundred free male inhabitants there shall be one representative, and so on progressively with the number of free male inhabitants, shall the right of representation increase, until the number of representatives shall amount to twenty-five, after which the number and proportion of representatives shall be regulated by the legislature; *provided* that no person be eligible or qualified to act as a representative, unless he shall have been a citizen of one of the United States three years and be a resident in the district, or unless he shall have resided in the district three years, and in either case shall likewise hold in his own right, in fee simple, two hundred acres of land within the same:—*Provided also,* that a freehold in fifty acres of land in the district, having been a citizen of one of the states, and being resident in the district; or the like freehold and two years residence in the district shall be necessary to qualify a man as an elector of a representative.

[Section 10.] The representatives thus elected, shall serve for the term of two years, and in case of the death of a representative, or removal from office, the governor shall issue a writ to the county or township for which he was a member, to elect another in his stead, to serve for the residue of the term.

[Section 11.] The general assembly, or legislature, shall consist of the governor, legislative council, and a house of representatives. The legislative council shall consist of five members, to continue in office five years, unless sooner removed by Congress, any three of whom to be a quorum, and the members of the council shall be nominated and appointed in the following manner, to wit: As soon as representatives shall be elected, the governor shall appoint a time and place for them to meet together, and, when met, they shall nominate ten persons, resident in the district, and each possessed of a freehold in five hundred acres of land, and return their names to Congress; five of whom Congress shall appoint and commission to serve as aforesaid; and whenever a vacancy shall happen in the council, by death or removal from office, the house of representatives shall nominate two persons, qualified as aforesaid, for each vacancy, and return their names to Congress; one of whom Congress shall appoint and commission for the residue of the term; and every five years, four months at least before the expiration of the time of service of the members of council, the said house shall nominate ten persons, qualified as aforesaid, and return their names to Congress, five of whom Congress shall appoint and commission to serve as members of the council five years, unless sooner removed. And the governor, legislative council, and house of representatives, shall have authority to make laws in all cases for the good government of the district, not repugnant to the principles and articles in this ordinance established and declared. And all bills having passed by a majority in the house, and by a majority in the council, shall be referred to the governor for his assent; but no bill or legislative act whatever, shall be of any force without his assent. The governor shall have power to convene, prorogue and dissolve the general assembly, when in his opinion it shall be expedient.

[Section 12.] The governor, judges, legislative council, secretary, and such other officers as Congress shall appoint in the district, shall take an oath or affirmation of fidelity, and of office, the governor before the president of Congress, and all other officers before the governor. As soon as a legislature shall be formed in the district, the council and house, assembled in one room, shall have authority by joint ballot to elect a delegate to Congress, who shall have a seat in Congress, with a right of debating, but not of voting, during this temporary government.

[Section 13.] And for extending the fundamental principles of civil and religious liberty, which form the basis whereon these republics, their laws and constitutions are erected; to fix and establish those principles as the basis of all laws, constitutions and governments, which for ever hereafter shall be formed in the said territory; —-to provide also for the establishment of states, and permanent government therein, and for their admission to a share in the federal councils on an equal footing with the original states, at as early periods as may be consistent with the general interest:

[Section 14.] It is hereby ordained and declared by the authority aforesaid, That the following articles shall be considered as articles of compact between the original states and the people and states in the said territory, and forever remain unalterable, unless by common consent, to wit:

Article the First. No person, demeaning himself in a peaceable and orderly manner, shall ever be molested on account of his mode of worship or religious sentiments in the said territory.

Article the Second. The inhabitants of the said territory shall always be entitled to the benefits of the writ of *habeas corpus,* and of the trial by jury; of a proportionate representation of the people in the legislature, and of judicial proceedings according to the course of the common law; all persons shall be bailable unless for capital offenses, where the proof shall be evident, or the presumption great; all fines shall be moderate, and no cruel or unusual punishments shall be inflicted; no man shall be deprived of his liberty or property but by the judgment of his peers, or the law of the land; and should the public exigencies make it necessary for the common preservation to take any person's property, or to demand his particular services, full compensation shall be made for the same; —-and in the just preservation of rights and property it is understood and declared, that no law ought ever to be made, or have force in the said territory, that shall in any manner whatever interfere with, or affect private contracts or engagements, *bona fide* and without fraud previously formed.

Article the Third. Religion, morality and knowledge, being necessary to good government and the happiness of mankind, schools and the means of education shall forever be encouraged. The utmost good faith shall always be observed towards the Indians; their lands and property shall never be taken from them without their consent; and in their property, rights and liberty, they never shall be invaded or disturbed, unless in just and lawful wars authorized by Congress; but laws founded in justice and humanity shall from time to time be made, for preventing wrongs being done to them; and for preserving peace and friendship with them.

Article the Fourth. The said territory, and the states which may be formed therein, shall forever remain a part of this confederacy of the United States of America, subject to the articles of confederation, and to such alterations therein as shall be constitutionally made; and to all the acts and ordinances of the United States in Congress assembled, conformable thereto. The inhabitants and settlers in the said territory, shall be subject to pay a part of the federal debts contracted or to be contracted, and a proportional part of the expences of government, to be apportioned on them by Congress, according to the same common rule and measure by which apportionments thereof shall be made on the other states; and the taxes for paying their proportion, shall be laid and levied by the authority and direction of the legislatures of the district or districts or new states, as in the original states, within the time agreed upon by the United States in Congress assembled. The legislatures of those districts, or new states, shall never interfere with the primary disposal of the soil by the United States in Congress assembled, nor with any regulations Congress may find necessary for securing the title in such soil to the *bona fide* purchasers. No tax shall be imposed on lands the property of the United States; and in no case shall non-resident proprietors be taxed higher than residents. The navigable waters leading into the Mississippi and St. Lawrence, and the carrying places between the same shall be common highways, and forever free, as well to the inhabitants of the said territory, as to the citizens of the United States, and those of any other states that may be admitted into the confederacy, without any tax, impost or duty therefor.

Article the Fifth. There shall be formed in the said territory, not less than three nor more than five states; and the boundaries of the states, as soon as Virginia shall alter her act of cession and consent to the same, shall become fixed and established as follows, to wit: The western state in the said territory, shall be bounded by the Mississippi, the Ohio and Wabash rivers; a direct line drawn from the Wabash and Post Vincent's due north to the territorial line between the United States and Canada, and by the said territorial line to the lake of the Woods and Mississippi. The middle state shall be bounded by the said direct line, the Wabash from Post Vincent's to the Ohio; by the Ohio, by a direct line drawn due north from the mouth of the Great Miami to the said territorial line, and by the said territorial line. The eastern state shall be bounded by the last mentioned direct line, the Ohio, Pennsylvania, and the said territorial line; *Provided however,* and it is further understood and declared, that the boundaries of these three states, shall be subject so far to be altered, that if Congress shall hereafter find it expedient, they shall have authority to form one or two states in that part of the said territory which lies north of an east and west line drawn through the southerly bend or extreme of lake Michigan: and whenever any of the said states shall have sixty thousand free inhabitants therein, such state shall be admitted by its delegates into the Congress of the United States, on an equal footing with the original states in all respects whatever; and shall be at liberty to form a permanent constitution and state government: *Provided* the constitution and government so to be formed, shall be republican, and in conformity to the principles contained in these articles, and so far as it can be consistent with the general interest of the confederacy, such admission shall be allowed at an earlier period, and when there may be a less number of free inhabitants in the state than sixty thousand.

Article the Sixth. There shall be neither slavery nor involuntary servitude in the said territory, otherwise than in punishment of crimes whereof the party shall have been duly convicted: *Provided always,* that any person escaping into the same, from whom labor or service is lawfully claimed in any one of the original states, such fugitive may be lawfully reclaimed and conveyed to the person claiming his or her labor or service as aforesaid.

Be it ordained by the authority aforesaid, That the resolutions of the 23d of April, 1784, relative to the subject of this ordinance, be, and the same are hereby repealed and declared null and void.

DONE by the UNITED STATES in CONGRESS assembled, the 13th day of July, in the year of our Lord 1787, and of their sovereignty and independence the 12th.

CONSTITUTION OF THE
UNITED STATES OF AMERICA (1787)[5]

We the People of the United States, in Order to form a more perfect
Union, establish Justice, insure domestic Tranquility, provide for

---

5. This text of the Constitution follows the engrossed copy signed by Gen.
Washington and the deputies from 12 States. . . .

In May 1785, a committee of Congress made a report recommending an
alteration in the Articles of Confederation, but no action was taken on it, and it
was left to the State Legislatures to proceed in the matter. In January 1786, the
Legislature of Virginia passed a resolution providing for the appointment of five
commissioners, who, or any three of them, should meet such commissioners as
might be appointed in the other States of the Union, at a time and place to be
agreed upon, to take into consideration the trade of the United States; to consider
how far a uniform system in their commercial regulations may be necessary to
their common interest and their permanent harmony; and to report to the several
States such an act, relative to this great object, as, when ratified by them, will
enable the United States in Congress effectually to provide for the same. The Virginia commissioners, after some correspondence, fixed the first Monday in September as the time, and the city of Annapolis as the place for the meeting, but
only four other States were represented, viz: Delaware, New York, New Jersey,
and Pennsylvania; the commissioners appointed by Massachusetts, New Hampshire, North Carolina, and Rhode Island failed to attend. Under the circumstances

the common defence, promote the general Welfare, and secure the Blessings of Liberty to ourselves and our Posterity, do ordain and establish this Constitution for the United States of America.

---

of so partial a representation, the commissioners present agreed upon a report, (drawn by Mr. Hamilton, of New York,) expressing their unanimous conviction that it might essentially tend to advance the interests of the Union if the States by which they were respectively delegated would concur, and use their endeavors to procure the concurrence of the other States, in the appointment of commissioners to meet at Philadelphia on the Second Monday of May following, to take into consideration the situation of the United States; to devise such further provisions as should appear to them necessary to render the Constitution of the Federal Government adequate to the exigencies of the Union; and to report such an act for that purpose to the United States in Congress assembled as, when agreed to by them and afterwards confirmed by the Legislatures of every State, would effectually provide for the same.

Congress, on the 21st of February, 1787, adopted a resolution in favor of a convention, and the Legislatures of those States which had not already done so (with the exception of Rhode Island) promptly appointed delegates. On the 25th of May, seven States having convened, George Washington, of Virginia, was unanimously elected President, and the consideration of the proposed constitution was commenced. On the 17th of September, 1787, the Constitution as engrossed and agreed upon was signed by all the members present, except Mr. Gerry of Massachusetts, and Messrs. Mason and Randolph, of Virginia. The president of the convention transmitted it to Congress, with a resolution stating how the proposed Federal Government should be put in operation, and an explanatory letter. Congress, on the 28th of September, 1787, directed the Constitution so framed, with the resolutions and letter concerning the same, to "be transmitted to the several Legislatures in order to be submitted to a convention of delegates chosen in each State by the people thereof, in conformity to the resolves of the convention."

On the 4th of March, 1789, the day which had been fixed for commencing the operations of Government under the new Constitution, it had been ratified by the conventions chosen in each State to consider it, as follows: Delaware, December 7, 1787; Pennsylvania, December 12, 1787; New Jersey, December 18, 1787; Georgia, January 2, 1788; Connecticut, January 9, 1788; Massachusetts, February 6, 1788; Maryland, April 28, 1788; South Carolina, May 23, 1788; New Hampshire, June 21, 1788; Virginia, June 25, 1788; and New York, July 26, 1788.

The President informed Congress, on the 28th of January, 1790, that North Carolina had ratified the Constitution November 21, 1789; and he informed Congress on the 1st of June, 1790, that Rhode Island had ratified the Constitution May 29, 1790. Vermont, in convention, ratified the Constitution January 10,

Article. I.

Section. 1. All legislative Powers herein granted shall be vested in a Congress of the United States, which shall consist of a Senate and a House of Representatives.

Section. 2. The House of Representatives shall be composed of Members chosen every second Year by the People of the several States, and the Electors in each State shall have the Qualifications requisite for Electors of the most numerous Branch of the State Legislature.

No person shall be a Representative who shall not have attained to the Age of twenty five Years, and been seven Years a Citizen of the United States, and who shall not, when elected, be an Inhabitant of that State in which he shall be chosen.

Representatives and direct Taxes shall be apportioned among the several States which may be included within this Union, according to their respective Numbers, which shall be determined by adding to the whole Number of free Persons, including those bound to Service for a Term of Years, and excluding Indians not taxed, three fifths of all other Persons.[6] The actual Enumeration shall be made within three Years after the first Meeting of the Congress of the United States, and within every subsequent Term of ten Years, in such Manner as they shall by Law direct. The Number of Representatives shall not exceed one for every thirty Thousand, but each State shall have at Least one Representative; and until such enumeration shall be made, the State of New Hampshire shall be entitled to chuse [*sic*] three, Massachusetts eight, Rhode-Island and Providence Plantations one, Connecticut five, New-York six, New Jersey four, Pennsylvania eight, Delaware one, Maryland six, Virginia ten, North Carolina five, South Carolina five, and Georgia three.

1791, and was, by an act of Congress approved February 18, 1791, "received and admitted into this Union as a new and entire member of the United States."

6. The part of this clause relating to the mode of apportionment of representatives among the several States has been affected by section 2 of amendment XIV, and as to taxes on incomes without apportionment by amendment XVI.

When vacancies happen in the Representation from any State, the Executive Authority thereof shall issue Writs of Election to fill such Vacancies.

The House of Representatives shall chuse their Speaker and other Officers; and shall have the sole Power of Impeachment.

Section. 3. The Senate of the United States shall be composed of two Senators from each State, chosen by the Legislature thereof,[7] for six Years; and each Senator shall have one Vote.

Immediately after they shall be assembled in Consequence of the first Election, they shall be divided as equally as may be into three Classes. The Seats of the Senators of the first Class shall be vacated at the Expiration of the second Year, of the second Class at the Expiration of the fourth Year, and of the third Class at the Expiration of the sixth Year, so that one third may be chosen every second Year; and if Vacancies happen by Resignation, or otherwise, during the Recess of the Legislature of any State, the Executive thereof may make temporary Appointments until the next Meeting of the Legislature, which shall then fill such Vacancies.[8]

No Person shall be a Senator who shall not have attained to the Age of thirty Years, and been nine Years a Citizen of the United States, and who shall not, when elected, be an Inhabitant of that State for which he shall be chosen.

The Vice President of the United States shall be President of the Senate, but shall have no Vote, unless they be equally divided.

The Senate shall chuse their other Officers, and also a President pro tempore, in the Absence of the Vice President, or when he shall exercise the Office of President of the United States.

The Senate shall have the sole Power to try all Impeachments. When sitting for that Purpose, they shall be on Oath or Affirmation. When the President of the United States is tried, the Chief Justice shall preside: And no Person shall be convicted without the Concurrence of two thirds of the Members present.

---

7. This clause has been affected by clause 1 of Amendment XVII.
8. This clause has been affected by clause 2 of Amendment XVIII.

Judgment in Cases of Impeachment shall not extend further than to removal from Office, and disqualification to hold and enjoy any Office of honor, Trust or Profit under the United States: but the Party convicted shall nevertheless be liable and subject to Indictment, Trial, Judgment and Punishment, according to Law.

Section. 4. The Times, Places and Manner of holding Elections for Senators and Representatives, shall be prescribed in each State by the Legislature thereof; but the Congress may at any time by Law make or alter such Regulations, except as to the Places of chusing Senators.

The Congress shall assemble at least once in every Year, and such Meeting shall be on the first Monday in December,[9] unless they shall by Law appoint a different Day.

Section. 5. Each House shall be the Judge of the Elections, Returns and Qualifications of its own Members, and a Majority of each shall constitute a Quorum to do Business; but a smaller Number may adjourn from day to day, and may be authorized to compel the Attendance of absent Members, in such Manner, and under such Penalties as each House may provide.

Each House may determine the Rules of its Proceedings, punish its Members for disorderly Behaviour, and, with the Concurrence of two thirds, expel a Member.

Each House shall keep a Journal of its Proceedings, and from time to time publish the same, excepting such Parts as may in their Judgment require Secrecy; and the Yeas and Nays of the Members of either House on any question shall, at the Desire of one fifth of those Present, be entered on the Journal.

Neither House, during the Session of Congress, shall, without the Consent of the other, adjourn for more than three days, nor to any other Place than that in which the two Houses shall be sitting.

Section. 6. The Senators and Representatives shall receive a Compensation for their Services, to be ascertained by Law, and

---

9. This clause has been affected by Amendment XX.

paid out of the Treasury of the United States.[10] They shall in all Cases, except Treason, Felony and Breach of the Peace, be privileged from Arrest during their Attendance at the Session of their respective Houses, and in going to and returning from the same; and for any Speech or Debate in either House, they shall not be questioned in any other Place.

No Senator or Representative shall, during the Time for which he was elected, be appointed to any civil Office under the Authority of the United States, which shall have been created, or the Emoluments whereof shall have been encreased during such time; and no Person holding any Office under the United States, shall be a Member of either House during his Continuance in Office.

Section. 7. All Bills for raising Revenue shall originate in the House of Representatives; but the Senate may propose or concur with Amendments as on other Bills.

Every Bill which shall have passed the House of Representatives and the Senate, shall, before it become a Law, be presented to the President of the United States; If he approve he shall sign it, but if not he shall return it, with his Objections to that House in which it shall have originated, who shall enter the Objections at large on their Journal, and proceed to reconsider it. If after such Reconsideration two thirds of that House shall agree to pass the Bill, it shall be sent, together with the Objections, to the other House, by which it shall likewise be reconsidered, and if approved by two thirds of that House, it shall become a Law. But in all such Cases the Votes of both Houses shall be determined by yeas and Nays, and the Names of the Persons voting for and against the Bill shall be entered on the Journal of each House respectively. If any Bill shall not be returned by the President within ten Days (Sundays excepted) after it shall have been presented to him, the Same shall be a Law, in like Manner as if he had signed it, unless the Congress by their Adjournment prevent its Return in which Case it shall not be a Law.

---

10. This clause has been affected by Amendment XXVII.

Every Order, Resolution, or Vote to which the Concurrence of the Senate and House of Representatives may be necessary (except on a question of Adjournment) shall be presented to the President of the United States; and before the Same shall take Effect, shall be approved by him, or being disapproved by him, shall be repassed by two thirds of the Senate and House of Representatives, according to the Rules and Limitations prescribed in the Case of a Bill.

Section. 8. The Congress shall have Power To lay and collect Taxes, Duties, Imposts and Excises, to pay the Debts and provide for the common Defence and general Welfare of the United States; but all Duties, Imposts and Excises shall be uniform throughout the United States;

To borrow Money on the credit of the United States;

To regulate Commerce with foreign Nations, and among the several States, and with the Indian Tribes;

To establish an uniform Rule of Naturalization, and uniform Laws on the subject of Bankruptcies throughout the United States;

To coin Money, regulate the Value thereof, and of foreign Coin, and fix the Standard of Weights and Measures;

To provide for the Punishment of counterfeiting the Securities and current Coin of the United States;

To establish Post Offices and post Roads;

To promote the Progress of Science and useful Arts, by securing for limited Times to Authors and Inventors the exclusive Right to their respective Writings and Discoveries;

To constitute Tribunals inferior to the supreme Court;

To define and punish Piracies and Felonies committed on the high Seas, and Offences against the Law of Nations;

To declare War, grant Letters of Marque and Reprisal, and make Rules concerning Captures on Land and Water;

To raise and support Armies, but no Appropriation of Money to that Use shall be for a longer Term than two Years;

To provide and maintain a Navy;

To make Rules for the Government and Regulation of the land and naval Forces;

To provide for calling forth the Militia to execute the Laws of the Union, suppress Insurrections and repel Invasions;

To provide for organizing, arming, and disciplining, the Militia, and for governing such Part of them as may be employed in the Service of the United States, reserving to the States respectively, the Appointment of the Officers, and the Authority of training the Militia according to the discipline prescribed by Congress;

To exercise exclusive Legislation in all Cases whatsoever, over such District (not exceeding ten Miles square) as may, by Cession of particular States, and the Acceptance of Congress, become the Seat of the Government of the United States, and to exercise like Authority over all Places purchased by the Consent of the Legislature of the State in which the Same shall be, for the Erection of Forts, Magazines, Arsenals, dock-Yards, and other needful Buildings;—And

To make all Laws which shall be necessary and proper for carrying into Execution the foregoing Powers, and all other Powers vested by this Constitution in the Government of the United States, or in any Department or Officer thereof.

Section. 9. The Migration or Importation of such Persons as any of the States now existing shall think proper to admit, shall not be prohibited by the Congress prior to the Year one thousand eight hundred and eight, but a Tax or duty may be imposed on such Importation, not exceeding ten dollars for each Person.

The Privilege of the Writ of Habeas Corpus shall not be suspended, unless when in Cases of Rebellion or Invasion the public Safety may require it.

No Bill of Attainder or ex post facto Law shall be passed.

No Capitation, or other direct, Tax shall be laid, unless in Proportion to the Census or Enumeration herein before directed to be taken.[11]

No Tax or Duty shall be laid on Articles exported from any State.

---

7. This clause has been affected by Amendment XVI.

No Preference shall be given by any Regulation of Commerce or Revenue to the Ports of one State over those of another: nor shall Vessels bound to, or from, one State, be obliged to enter, clear, or pay Duties in another.

No Money shall be drawn from the Treasury, but in Consequence of Appropriations made by Law; and a regular Statement and Account of the Receipts and Expenditures of all public Money shall be published from time to time.

No Title of Nobility shall be granted by the United States: And no Person holding any Office of Profit or Trust under them, shall, without the Consent of the Congress, accept of any present, Emolument, Office, or Title, of any kind whatever, from any King, Prince, or foreign State.

Section. 10. No State shall enter into any Treaty, Alliance, or Confederation; grant Letters of Marque and Reprisal; coin Money; emit Bills of Credit; make any Thing but gold and silver Coin a Tender in Payment of Debts; pass any Bill of Attainder, ex post facto Law, or Law impairing the Obligation of Contracts, or grant any Title of Nobility.

No State shall, without the Consent of the Congress, lay any Imposts or Duties on Imports or Exports, except what may be absolutely necessary for executing it's [*sic*] inspection Laws: and the net Produce of all Duties and Imposts, laid by any State on Imports or Exports, shall be for the Use of the Treasury of the United States; and all such Laws shall be subject to the Revision and Controul of the Congress.

No State shall, without the Consent of Congress, lay any Duty of Tonnage, keep Troops, or Ships of War in time of Peace, enter into any Agreement or Compact with another State, or with a foreign Power, or engage in War, unless actually invaded, or in such imminent Danger as will not admit of delay.

Article. II.

Section. 1. The executive Power shall be vested in a President of the United States of America. He shall hold his Office during the Term of four Years, and, together with the Vice President, chosen for the same Term, be elected, as follows

Each State shall appoint, in such Manner as the Legislature thereof may direct, a Number of Electors, equal to the whole Number of Senators and Representatives to which the State may be entitled in the Congress: but no Senator or Representative, or Person holding an Office of Trust or Profit under the United States, shall be appointed an Elector.

The Electors shall meet in their respective States, and vote by Ballot for two Persons, of whom one at least shall not be an Inhabitant of the same State with themselves. And they shall make a List of all the Persons voted for, and of the Number of Votes for each; which List they shall sign and certify, and transmit sealed to the Seat of the Government of the United States, directed to the President of the Senate. The President of the Senate shall, in the Presence of the Senate and House of Representatives, open all the Certificates, and the Votes shall then be counted. The Person having the greatest Number of Votes shall be the President, if such Number be a Majority of the whole Number of Electors appointed; and if there be more than one who have such Majority, and have an equal Number of Votes, then the House of Representatives shall immediately chuse by Ballot one of them for President; and if no Person have a Majority, then from the five highest on the List the said House shall in like Manner chuse the President. But in chusing the President, the Votes shall be taken by States, the Representation from each State having one Vote; A quorum for this Purpose shall consist of a Member or Members from two thirds of the States, and a Majority of all the States shall be necessary to a Choice. In every Case, after the Choice of the President, the Person having the greatest Number of Votes of the Electors shall be the Vice President. But if there should remain two or more who have equal Votes, the Senate shall chuse from them by Ballot the Vice President.[12]

The Congress may determine the Time of chusing the Electors, and the Day on which they shall give their Votes; which Day shall be the same throughout the United States.

No Person except a natural born Citizen, or a Citizen of the United States, at the time of the Adoption of this Constitution, shall be eligible to the Office of President; neither shall any person be eligible to that Office who shall not have attained to the Age of thirty five Years, and been fourteen Years a Resident within the United States.

In Case of the Removal of the President from Office, or of his Death, Resignation, or Inability to discharge the Powers and Duties of the said Office,[13] the Same shall devolve on the Vice President, and the Congress may by Law provide for the Case of Removal, Death, Resignation or Inability, both of the President and Vice President, declaring what Officer shall then act as President, and such Officer shall act accordingly, until the Disability be removed, or a President shall be elected.

The President shall, at stated Times, receive for his Services, a Compensation, which shall neither be encreased nor diminished during the Period for which he shall have been elected, and he shall not receive within that Period any other Emolument from the United States, or any of them.

Before he enter on the Execution of his Office, he shall take the following Oath or Affirmation:—"I do solemnly swear (or affirm) that I will faithfully execute the Office of President of the United States, and will to the best of my Ability, preserve, protect and defend the Constitution of the United States."

Section. 2. The President shall be Commander in Chief of the Army and Navy of the United States, and of the Militia of the sev-

---

12. This clause has been affected by Amendment XII.
13. This clause has been affected by Amendment XXV.

eral States, when called into the actual Service of the United States; he may require the Opinion, in writing, of the principal Officer in each of the executive Departments, upon any Subject relating to the Duties of their respective Offices, and he shall have Power to grant Reprieves and Pardons for Offences against the United States, except in Cases of Impeachment.

He shall have Power, by and with the Advice and Consent of the Senate, to make Treaties, provided two thirds of the Senators present concur; and he shall nominate, and by and with the Advice and Consent of the Senate, shall appoint Ambassadors, other public Ministers and Consuls, Judges of the supreme Court, and all other Officers of the United States, whose Appointments are not herein otherwise provided for, and which shall be established by Law: but the Congress may by Law vest the Appointment of such inferior Officers, as they think proper, in the President alone, in the Courts of Law, or in the Heads of Departments.

The President shall have Power to fill up all Vacancies that may happen during the Recess of the Senate, by granting Commissions which shall expire at the End of their next Session.

Section. 3. He shall from time to time give to the Congress Information of the State of the Union, and recommend to their Consideration such Measures as he shall judge necessary and expedient; he may, on extraordinary Occasions, convene both Houses, or either of them, and in Case of Disagreement between them, with Respect to the Time of Adjournment, he may adjourn them to such Time as he shall think proper; he shall receive Ambassadors and other public Ministers; he shall take Care that the Laws be faithfully executed, and shall Commission all the Officers of the United States.

Section. 4. The President, Vice President and all civil Officers of the United States, shall be removed from Office on Impeachment for, and Conviction of, Treason, Bribery, or other high Crimes and Misdemeanors.

Article. III.

Section. 1. The judicial Power of the United States, shall be vested in one supreme Court, and in such inferior Courts as the Congress may from time to time ordain and establish. The Judges, both of the supreme and inferior Courts, shall hold their Offices during good Behaviour, and shall, at stated Times, receive for their Services, a Compensation, which shall not be diminished during their Continuance in Office.

Section. 2. The judicial Power shall extend to all Cases, in Law and Equity, arising under this Constitution, the Laws of the United States, and Treaties made, or which shall be made, under their Authority;—to all Cases affecting Ambassadors, other public Ministers and Consuls;—to all Cases of admiralty and maritime Jurisdiction;—to Controversies to which the United States shall be a Party;—to Controversies between two or more States;—between a State and Citizens of another State;[14]—between Citizens of different States,—between Citizens of the same State claiming Lands under Grants of different States, and between a State, or the Citizens thereof, and foreign States, Citizens or Subjects.

In all Cases affecting Ambassadors, other public Ministers and Consuls, and those in which a State shall be a Party, the supreme Court shall have original Jurisdiction. In all the other Cases before mentioned, the supreme Court shall have appellate Jurisdiction, both as to Law and Fact, with such Exceptions, and under such Regulations as the Congress shall make.

The Trial of all Crimes, except in Cases of Impeachment, shall be by Jury; and such Trial shall be held in the State where the said Crimes shall have been committed; but when not committed within any State, the Trial shall be at such Place or Places as the Congress may by Law have directed.

Section. 3. Treason against the United States, shall consist only

---

14. This clause has been affected by Amendment XVI.

in levying War against them, or in adhering to their Enemies, giving them Aid and Comfort. No Person shall be convicted of Treason unless on the Testimony of two Witnesses to the same overt Act, or on Confession in open Court.

The Congress shall have Power to declare the Punishment of Treason, but no Attainder of Treason shall work Corruption of Blood, or Forfeiture except during the Life of the Person attainted.

Article. IV.

Section. 1. Full Faith and Credit shall be given in each State to the public Acts, Records, and judicial Proceedings of every other State. And the Congress may by general Laws prescribe the Manner in which such Acts, Records and Proceedings shall be proved, and the Effect thereof.

Section. 2. The Citizens of each State shall be entitled to all Privileges and Immunities of Citizens in the several States.

A Person charged in any State with Treason, Felony, or other Crime, who shall flee from Justice, and be found in another State, shall on Demand of the executive Authority of the State from which he fled, be delivered up, to be removed to the State having Jurisdiction of the Crime.

No Person held to Service or Labour in one State, under the Laws thereof, escaping into another, shall, in Consequence of any Law or Regulation therein, be discharged from such Service or Labour, but shall be delivered up on Claim of the Party to whom such Service or Labour may be due.[15]

Section. 3. New States may be admitted by the Congress into this Union; but no new State shall be formed or erected within the Jurisdiction of any other State; nor any State be formed by the Junction of two or more States, or Parts of States, without the Consent of the Legislatures of the States concerned as well as of the Congress.

---

15. This clause has been affected by amendment XIII.

The Congress shall have Power to dispose of and make all needful Rules and Regulations respecting the Territory or other Property belonging to the United States; and nothing in this Constitution shall be so construed as to Prejudice any Claims of the United States, or of any particular State.

Section. 4. The United States shall guarantee to every State in this Union a Republican Form of Government, and shall protect each of them against Invasion; and on Application of the Legislature, or of the Executive (when the Legislature cannot be convened) against domestic Violence.

Article. V.

The Congress, whenever two thirds of both Houses shall deem it necessary, shall propose Amendments to this Constitution, or, on the Application of the Legislatures of two thirds of the several States, shall call a Convention for proposing Amendments, which, in either Case, shall be valid to all Intents and Purposes, as Part of this Constitution, when ratified by the Legislatures of three fourths of the several States, or by Conventions in three fourths thereof, as the one or the other Mode of Ratification may be proposed by the Congress; Provided that no Amendment which may be made prior to the Year One thousand eight hundred and eight shall in any Manner affect the first and fourth Clauses in the Ninth Section of the first Article; and that no State, without its Consent, shall be deprived of it's [*sic*] equal Suffrage in the Senate.

Article. VI.

All Debts contracted and Engagements entered into, before the Adoption of this Constitution, shall be as valid against the United States under this Constitution, as under the Confederation.

This Constitution, and the Laws of the United States which shall be made in Pursuance thereof; and all Treaties made, or which shall be made, under the Authority of the United States, shall be the supreme Law of the Land; and the Judges in every State shall be bound thereby, any Thing in the Constitution or Laws of any State to the Contrary notwithstanding.

The Senators and Representatives before mentioned, and the Members of the several State Legislatures, and all executive and judicial Officers, both of the United States and of the several States, shall be bound by Oath or Affirmation, to support this Constitution; but no religious Test shall ever be required as a Qualification to any Office or public Trust under the United States.

Article. VII.

The Ratification of the Conventions of nine States, shall be sufficient for the Establishment of this Constitution between the States so ratifying the Same.

DONE in Convention by the Unanimous Consent of the States present the Seventeenth Day of September in the Year of our Lord one thousand seven hundred and Eighty seven and of the Independence of the United States of America the Twelfth. In WITNESS whereof We have hereunto subscribed our Names,

Go. Washington—*Presidt and deputy from Virginia*

[Signed also by the deputies of twelve States.]

New Hampshire

JOHN LANGDON   NICHOLAS GILMAN

Massachusetts

NATHANIEL GORHAM   RUFUS KING

Connecticut

WM. SAML. JOHNSON   ROGER SHERMAN

New York

ALEXANDER HAMILTON

New Jersey

WIL: LIVINGSTON   WM. PATERSON.
DAVID BREARLEY.   JONA: DAYTON

Pennsylvania

B FRANKLIN   THOS. FITZSIMONS
THOMAS MIFFLIN   JARED INGERSOLL
ROBT MORRIS   JAMES WILSON.
GEO. CLYMER   GOUV MORRIS

Delaware

GEO: READ   RICHARD BASSETT
GUNNING BEDFORD JUN   JACO: BROOM
JOHN DICKINSON

Maryland

JAMES MCHENRY   DANL. CARROLL.
DAN OF ST THOS. JENIFER

Virginia

JOHN BLAIR—   JAMES MADISON JR.

North Carolina

WM BLOUNT   HU WILLIAMSON
RICHD. DOBBS SPAIGHT

South Carolina

J. RUTLEDGE   CHARLES PINCKNEY
CHARLES COTESWORTH   PIERCE BUTLER.
    PINCKNEY

Georgia

WILLIAM FEW   ABR BALDWIN

Attest: WILLIAM JACKSON *Secretary*

ARTICLES IN ADDITION TO, AND AMENDMENT OF, THE CONSTITUTION OF THE UNITED STATES, PROPOSED BY CONGRESS AND RATIFIED BY THE SEVERAL STATES, PURSUANT TO THE FIFTH ARTICLE OF THE ORIGINAL CONSTITUTION[16]

---

16. The first ten amendments to the Constitution of the United States (and two others, one of which failed of ratification and the other which later became the 27th amendment) were proposed to the legislatures of the several States by the First Congress on September 25, 1789. The first ten amendments were ratified by the following States, and the notifications of ratification by the Governors thereof were successively communicated by the President to Congress: New Jersey, November 20, 1789; Maryland, December 19, 1789; North Carolina, December 22, 1789; South Carolina, January 19, 1790; New Hampshire, January 25, 1790; Delaware, January 28, 1790; New York, February 24, 1790; Pennsylvania, March 10, 1790; Rhode Island, June 7, 1790; Vermont, November 3, 1791; and Virginia, December 15, 1791.

Ratification was completed on December 15, 1791.

The amendments were subsequently ratified by the legislatures of Massachusetts, March 2, 1939; Georgia, March 18, 1939; and Connecticut, April 19, 1939.

Article {I} (1791)[17]

Congress shall make no law respecting an establishment of religion, or prohibiting the free exercise thereof; or abridging the freedom of speech, or of the press; or the right of the people peaceably to assemble, and to petition the Government for a redress of grievances.

Article {II} (1791)

A well regulated Militia, being necessary to the security of a free state, the right of the people to keep and bear Arms, shall not be infringed.

Article {III} (1791)

No Soldier shall, in time of peace be quartered in any house, without the consent of the Owner, nor in time of war, but in a manner to be prescribed by law.

Article {IV} (1791)

The right of the people to be secure in their persons, houses, papers, and effects, against unreasonable searches and seizures, shall not be violated, and no warrants shall issue, but upon probable cause, supported by Oath or affirmation, and particularly describing the place to be searched, and the persons or things to be seized.

Article {V} (1791)

No person shall be held to answer for a capital, or otherwise infamous crime, unless on a presentment or indictment of a Grand Jury,

17. Only the 13th, 14th, 15th, and 16th articles of amendment had numbers assigned to them at the time of ratification.

except in cases arising in the land or naval forces, or in the Militia, when in actual service in time of War or public danger; nor shall any person be subject for the same offence to be twice put in jeopardy of life or limb; nor shall be compelled in any criminal case to be a witness against himself, nor be deprived of life, liberty, or property, without due process of law; nor shall private property be taken for public use, without just compensation.

Article {VI} (1791)

In all criminal prosecutions, the accused shall enjoy the right to a speedy and public trial, by an impartial jury of the State and district wherein the crime shall have been committed, which district shall have been previously ascertained by law, and to be informed of the nature and cause of the accusation; to be confronted with the witnesses against him; to have compulsory process for obtaining witnesses in his favor, and to have the Assistance of Counsel for his defence.

Article {VII} (1791)

In Suits at common law, where the value in controversy shall exceed twenty dollars, the right of trial by jury shall be preserved, and no fact tried by a jury, shall be otherwise re-examined in any Court of the United States, than according to the rules of the common law.

Article {VIII} (1791)

Excessive bail shall not be required, nor excessive fines imposed, nor cruel and unusual punishments inflicted.

Article {IX} (1791)

The enumeration in the Constitution, of certain rights, shall not be construed to deny or disparage others retained by the people.

Article {X} (1791)

The powers not delegated to the United States by the Constitution, nor prohibited by it to the States, are reserved to the States respectively, or to the people.

Article {XI} (1798)[18]

The Judicial power of the United States shall not be construed to extend to any suit in law or equity, commenced or prosecuted against one of the United States by Citizens of another State, or by Citizens or Subjects of any Foreign State.

Article {XII} (1804)

The Electors shall meet in their respective states, and vote by ballot for President and Vice-President, one of whom, at least, shall not be an inhabitant of the same state with themselves; they shall name in their ballots the person voted for as President, and in distinct ballots the person voted for as Vice-President, and they shall make distinct lists of all persons voted for as President, and of all persons voted for as Vice-President, and of the number of votes for each, which lists they shall sign and certify, and transmit sealed to the seat of the government of the United States, directed to the President of the Senate;—The President of the Senate shall, in the presence of the Senate and House of Representatives, open all the certificates and the votes shall then be counted;—The person having the greatest number of votes for President, shall be the President, if such number be a majority of the whole number of Electors appointed; and if no

---

18. [Beginning with Article XI of the Amendments, the text of the Constitution in the "Organic Laws" section of the *United States Code* appends a paragraph titled "Proposal and Ratification" to the text of all the Amendments. Except for Articles XIII, XIV, and XV—the Civil War Amendments—that paragraph has been omitted in this book's text of the Constitution.]

person have such majority, then from the persons having the highest numbers not exceeding three on the list of those voted for as President, the House of Representatives shall choose immediately, by ballot, the President. But in choosing the President, the votes shall be taken by states, the representation from each state having one vote; a quorum for this purpose shall consist of a member or members from two-thirds of the states, and a majority of all the states shall be necessary to a choice. And if the House of Representatives shall not choose a President whenever the right of choice shall devolve upon them, before the fourth day of March next following, then the Vice-President shall act as President, as in the case of the death or other constitutional disability of the President.[19]—The person having the greatest number of votes as Vice-President, shall be the Vice-President, if such number be a majority of the whole number of Electors appointed, and if no person have a majority, then from the two highest numbers on the list, the Senate shall choose the Vice-President; a quorum for the purpose shall consist of two-thirds of the whole number of Senators, and a majority of the whole number shall be necessary to a choice. But no person constitutionally ineligible to the office of President shall be eligible to that of Vice-President of the United States.

Article {XIII} (1865)

Section 1. Neither slavery nor involuntary servitude, except as a punishment for crime whereof the party shall have been duly convicted, shall exist within the United States, or any place subject to their jurisdiction.

Section 2. Congress shall have power to enforce this article by appropriate legislation.

---

19. This sentence has been superseded by section 3 of Amendment XX.

PROPOSAL AND RATIFICATION

The thirteenth amendment to the Constitution of the United States was proposed to the legislatures of the several States by the Thirty-eighth Congress, on the 31st day of January, 1865, and was declared, in a proclamation of the Secretary of State, dated the 18th of December, 1865, to have been ratified by the legislatures of twenty-seven of the thirty-six States. The dates of ratification were: Illinois, February 1, 1865; Rhode Island, February 2, 1865; Michigan, February 2, 1865; Maryland, February 3, 1865; New York, February 3, 1865; Pennsylvania, February 3, 1865; West Virginia, February 3, 1865; Missouri, February 6, 1865; Maine, February 7, 1865; Kansas, February 7, 1865; Massachusetts, February 7, 1865; Virginia, February 9, 1865; Ohio, February 10, 1865; Indiana, February 13, 1865; Nevada, February 16, 1865; Louisiana, February 17, 1865; Minnesota, February 23, 1865; Wisconsin, February 24, 1865; Vermont, March 9, 1865; Tennessee, April 7, 1865; Arkansas, April 14, 1865; Connecticut, May 4, 1865; New Hampshire, July 1, 1865; South Carolina, November 13, 1865; Alabama, December 2, 1865; North Carolina, December 4, 1865; Georgia, December 6, 1865.

Ratification was completed on December 6, 1865.

The amendment was subsequently ratified by Oregon, December 8, 1865; California, December 19, 1865; Forida, December 28, 1865 (Florida again ratified on June 9, 1868, upon its adoption of a new constitution); Iowa, January 15, 1866; New Jersey, January 23, 1866 (after having rejected the amendment on March 16, 1865); Texas, February 18, 1870; Delaware, February 12, 1901 (after having rejected the amendment on February 8, 1865); Kentucky, March 18, 1976 (after having rejected it on February 24, 1865).

The amendment was rejected (and not subsequently ratified) by Mississippi, December 4, 1865.

Article {XIV} (1868)

Section 1. All persons born or naturalized in the United States, and subject to the jurisdiction thereof, are citizens of the United States and of the State wherein they reside. No State shall make or enforce any law which shall abridge the privileges or immunities of citizens of the United States; nor shall any State deprive any person of life, liberty, or property, without due process of law; nor deny to any person within its jurisdiction the equal protection of the laws.

Section 2. Representatives shall be apportioned among the several States according to their respective numbers, counting the whole number of persons in each State, excluding Indians not taxed. But when the right to vote at any election for the choice of electors for President and Vice President of the United States, Representatives in Congress, the Executive and Judicial officers of a State, or the members of the Legislature thereof, is denied to any of the male inhabitants of such State, being twenty-one years of age,[20] and citizens of the United States, or in any way abridged, except for participation in rebellion, or other crime, the basis of representation therein shall be reduced in the proportion which the number of such male citizens shall bear to the whole number of male citizens twenty-one years of age in such State.

Section 3. No person shall be a Senator or Representative in Congress, or elector of President and Vice President, or hold any office, civil or military, under the United States, or under any State, who, having previously taken an oath, as a member of Congress, or as an officer of the United States, or as a member of any State legislature, or as an executive or judicial officer of any State, to support the Constitution of the United States, shall have engaged in insurrection or rebellion against the same, or given aid or comfort to the enemies thereof. But Congress may by a vote of two-thirds of each House, remove such disability.

Section 4. The validity of the public debt of the United States, authorized by law, including debts incurred for payment of pensions and bounties for services in suppressing insurrection or rebellion, shall not be questioned. But neither the United States nor any

---

20. See Amendment XIX and section 1 of Amendment XXVI.

State shall assume or pay any debt or obligation incurred in aid of insurrection or rebellion against the United States, or any claim for the loss or emancipation of any slave; but all such debts, obligations and claims shall be held illegal and void.

Section 5. The Congress shall have power to enforce, by appropriate legislation, the provisions of this article.

PROPOSAL AND RATIFICATION

The fourteenth amendment to the Constitution of the United States was proposed to the legislatures of the several States by the Thirty-ninth Congress, on the 13th of June, 1866. It was declared, in a certificate of the Secretary of State dated July 28, 1868 to have been ratified by the legislatures of 28 of the 37 States. The dates of ratification were: Connecticut, June 25, 1866; New Hampshire, July 6, 1866; Tennessee, July 19, 1866; New Jersey, September 11, 1866 (subsequently the legislature rescinded its ratification, and on March 24, 1868, readopted its resolution of rescission over the Governor's veto, and on Nov. 12, 1980, expressed support for the amendment); Oregon, September 19, 1866 (and rescinded its ratification on October 15, 1868); Vermont, October 30, 1866; Ohio, January 4, 1867 (and rescinded its ratification on January 15, 1868); New York, January 10, 1867; Kansas, January 11, 1867; Illinois, January 15, 1867; West Virginia, January 16, 1867; Michigan, January 16, 1867; Minnesota, January 16, 1867; Maine, January 19, 1867; Nevada, January 22, 1867; Indiana, January 23, 1867; Missouri, January 25, 1867; Rhode Island, February 7, 1867; Wisconsin, February 7, 1867; Pennsylvania, February 12, 1867; Massachusetts, March 20, 1867; Nebraska, June 15, 1867; Iowa, March 16, 1868; Arkansas, April 6, 1868; Florida, June 9, 1868; North Carolina, July 4, 1868 (after having rejected it on December 14, 1866); Louisiana, July 9, 1868 (after having rejected it on February 6, 1867); South Carolina, July 9, 1868 (after having rejected it on December 20, 1866).

Ratification was completed on July 9, 1868.

The amendment was subsequently ratified by Alabama, July

13, 1868; Georgia, July 21, 1868 (after having rejected It, on November 9, 1866); Virginia, October 8, 1869 (after having rejected it on January 9, 1867); Mississippi, January 17, 1870; Texas, February 18, 1870 (after having rejected it on October 27, 1866); Delaware, February 12, 1901 (after having rejected it on February 8, 1867); Maryland, April 4, 1959 (after having rejected it on March 23, 1867); California, May 6, 1959; Kentucky, March 18, 1976 (after having rejected it. on January 8, 1867).

Article {XV} (1870)

Section 1. The right of citizens of the United States to vote shall not be denied or abridged by the United States or by any State on account of race, color, or previous condition of servitude.

Section 2. The Congress shall have power to enforce this article by appropriate legislation.

PROPOSAL AND RATIFICATION

The fifteenth amendment to the Constitution of the United States was proposed to the legislatures of the several States by the Fortieth Congress, on the 26th of February, 1869, and was declared, in a proclamation of the Secretary of State, dated March 30, 1870, to have been ratified by the legislatures of twenty-nine of the thirty-seven States. The dates of ratification were: Nevada, March 1, 1869; West Virginia, March 3, 1869; Illinois, March 5, 1869; Louisiana, March 5, 1869; North Carolina, March 5, 1869; Michigan, March 8, 1869; Wisconsin, March 9, 1869; Maine, March 11, 1869; Massachusetts, March 12, 1869; Arkansas, March 15, 1869; South Carolina, March 15, 1869; Pennsylvania, March 25, 1869; New York, April 14, 1869 (and the legislature of the same State passed a resolution January 5, 1870, to withdraw its consent to it, which action it rescinded on March 30, 1970); Indiana, May 14, 1869; Connecticut, May 19, 1869; Florida, June 14, 1869; New Hampshire, July 1, 1869; Virginia, October 8, 1869; Vermont, October 20, 1869; Missouri, January 7, 1870;

Minnesota, January 13, 1870; Mississippi, January 17, 1870; Rhode Island, January 18, 1870; Kansas, January 19, 1870; Ohio, January 27, 1870 (after having rejected it on April 30, 1869); Georgia, February 2, 1870; Iowa, February 3, 1870.

Ratification was completed on February 3, 1870, unless the withdrawal of ratification by New York was effective; in which event ratification was completed on February 17, 1870, when Nebraska ratified.

The amendment was subsequently ratified by Texas, February 18, 1870; New Jersey, February 15, 1871 (after having rejected it on February 7, 1870); Delaware, February 12, 1901 (after having rejected it on March 18, 1869); Oregon, February 24, 1959; California, April 3, 1962 (after having rejected it on January 28, 1870); Kentucky, March 18, 1976 (after having rejected it on March 12, 1869).

The amendment was approved by the Governor of Maryland, May 7, 1973; Maryland having previously rejected it on February 26, 1870.

The amendment was rejected (and not subsequently ratified) by Tennessee, November 16, 1869.

Article {XVI} (1913)

The Congress shall have power to lay and collect taxes on incomes, from whatever source derived, without apportionment among the several States, and without regard to any census or enumeration.

Article {XVII} (1913)

The Senate of the United States shall be composed of two Senators from each State, elected by the people thereof, for six years; and each Senator shall have one vote. The electors in each State shall have the qualifications requisite for electors of the most numerous branch of the State legislatures.

When vacancies happen in the representation of any State in the

Senate, the executive authority of such State shall issue writs of election to fill such vacancies: *Provided,* That the legislature of any State may empower the executive thereof to make temporary appointments until the people fill the vacancies by election as the legislature may direct.

This amendment shall not be so construed as to affect the election or term of any Senator chosen before it becomes valid as part of the Constitution.

Article {XVIII} (1919)[21]

Section 1. After one year from the ratification of this article the manufacture, sale, or transportation of intoxicating liquors within, the importation thereof into, or the exportation thereof from the United States and all territory subject to the jurisdiction thereof for beverage purposes is hereby prohibited.

Sec. 2. The Congress and the several States shall have concurrent power to enforce this article by appropriate legislation.

Sec. 3. This article shall be inoperative unless it shall have been ratified as an amendment to the Constitution by the legislatures of the several States, as provided in the Constitution, within seven years from the date of the submission hereof to the States by the Congress.

Article {XIX} (1920)

The right of citizens of the United States to vote shall not be denied or abridged by the United States or by any State on account of sex.

Congress shall have power to enforce this article by appropriate legislation.

---

21. Repealed by section 1 of Amendment XXI.

Article {XX} (1933)

Section 1. The terms of the President and Vice President shall end at noon on the 20th day of January, and the terms of Senators and Representatives at noon on the 3d day of January, of the years in which such terms would have ended if this article had not been ratified; and the terms of their successors shall then begin.

Sec. 2. The Congress shall assemble at least once in every year, and such meeting shall begin at noon on the 3d day of January, unless they shall by law appoint a different day.

Sec. 3. If, at the time fixed for the beginning of the term of the President, the President elect shall have died, the Vice President elect shall become President. If a President shall not have been chosen before the time fixed for the beginning of his term, or if the President elect shall have failed to qualify, then the Vice President elect shall act as President until a President shall have qualified; and the Congress may by law provide for the case wherein neither a President elect nor a Vice President elect shall have qualified, declaring who shall then act as President, or the manner in which one who is to act shall be selected, and such person shall act accordingly until a President or Vice President shall have qualified.

Sec. 4. The Congress may by law provide for the case of the death of any of the persons from whom the House of Representatives may choose a President whenever the right of choice shall have devolved upon them, and for the case of the death of any of the persons from whom the Senate may choose a Vice President whenever the right of choice shall have devolved upon them.

Sec. 5. Sections 1 and 2 shall take effect on the 15th day of October following the ratification of this article.

Sec. 6. This article shall be inoperative unless it shall have been ratified as an amendment to the Constitution by the legislatures of three-fourths of the several States within seven years from the date of its submission.

Article {XXI} (1933)

Section 1. The eighteenth article of amendment to the Constitution of the United States is hereby repealed.

Sec. 2. The transportation or importation into any State, Territory, or possession of the United States for delivery or use therein of intoxicating liquors, in violation of the laws thereof, is hereby prohibited.

Sec. 3. This article shall be inoperative unless it shall have been ratified as an amendment to the Constitution by conventions in the several States, as provided in the Constitution, within seven years from the date of the submission hereof to the States by the Congress.

Article {XXII} (1951)

Section 1. No person shall be elected to the office of the President more than twice, and no person who has held the office of President, or acted as President, for more than two years of a term to which some other person was elected President shall be elected to the office of the President more than once. But this Article shall not apply to any person holding the office of President when this Article was proposed by the Congress, and shall not prevent any person who may be holding the office of President, or acting as President, during the term within which this Article becomes operative from holding the office of President or acting as President during the remainder of such term.

Sec. 2. This article shall be inoperative unless it shall have been ratified as an amendment to the Constitution by the legislatures of three-fourths of the several States within seven years from the date of its submission to the States by the Congress.

Article {XXIII} (1961)

Section 1. The District constituting the seat of Government of the United States shall appoint in such manner as the Congress may direct:

A number of electors of President and Vice President equal to the whole number of Senators and Representatives in Congress to which the District would be entitled if it were a State, but in no event more than the least populous State; they shall be in addition to those appointed by the States, but they shall be considered, for the purposes of the election of President and Vice President, to be electors appointed by a State; and they shall meet in the District and perform such duties as provided by the twelfth article of amendment.

Section 2. The Congress shall have power to enforce this article by appropriate legislation.

Article {XXIV} (1964)

Section 1. The right of citizens of the United States to vote in any primary or other election for President or Vice President, for electors for President or Vice President, or for Senator or Representative in Congress, shall not be denied or abridged by the United States or any State by reason of failure to pay any poll tax or other tax.

Section 2. The Congress shall have power to enforce this article by appropriate legislation.

Article {XXV} (1967)

Section 1. In case of the removal of the President from office or of his death or resignation, the Vice President shall become President.

Sec. 2. Whenever there is a vacancy in the office of the Vice President, the President shall nominate a Vice President who shall take office upon confirmation by a majority vote of both Houses of Congress.

Sec. 3. Whenever the President transmits to the President pro tempore of the Senate and the Speaker of the House of Representatives his written declaration that he is unable to discharge the powers and duties of his office, and until he transmits to them a written declaration to the contrary, such powers and duties shall be discharged by the Vice President as Acting President.

Sec. 4. Whenever the Vice President and a majority of either the principal officers of the executive departments or of such other body as Congress may by law provide, transmit to the President pro tempore of the Senate and the Speaker of the House of Representatives their written declaration that the President is unable to discharge the powers and duties of his office, the Vice President shall immediately assume the powers and duties of the office as Acting President.

Thereafter, when the President transmits to the President pro tempore of the Senate and the Speaker of the House of Representatives his written declaration that no inability exists, he shall resume the powers and duties of his office unless the Vice President and a majority of either the principal officers of the executive department[22] or of such other body as Congress may by law provide, transmit within four days to the President pro tempore of the Senate and the Speaker of the House of Representatives their written declaration that the President is unable to discharge the powers and duties of his office. Thereupon Congress shall decide the issue, assembling within forty-eight hours for that purpose if not in session. If the Congress, within twenty-one days after receipt of the latter written declaration, or, if Congress is not in session, within twenty-one days after Congress is required to assemble, determines by two-thirds vote of both Houses that the President is unable to discharge the powers and duties of his office, the Vice President shall continue to discharge the same as Acting President; otherwise, the President shall resume the powers and duties of his office.

---

22. So in original. Probably should be "departments."

Article {XXVI} (1971)

Sec. 1. The right of citizens of the United States, who are eighteen years of age or older, to vote shall not be denied or abridged by the United States or by any State on account of age.

Sec. 2. The Congress shall have power to enforce this article by appropriate legislation.

Article {XXVII} (1992)[23]

No law, varying the compensation for the services of the Senators and Representatives, shall take effect, until an election of Representatives shall have intervened.

---

23. [Following the text of Article XXVII of the Amendments in the "Organic Laws" section of the *United States Code* is a section titled "Proposed Amendments to the Constitution Not Ratified by the States." That section has been omitted in this book's text of the Constitution.]

Suggested Reading

Abraham, Henry J. *The Judiciary: The Supreme Court in the Governmental Process.* New York: New York University Press, 1996.

Anastaplo, George. *The Constitution of 1787: A Commentary.* Baltimore and London: The Johns Hopkins University Press, 1989.

———. *The Amendments to the Constitution: A Commentary.* Baltimore: The Johns Hopkins University Press, 1995.

American Enterprise Institute for Public Policy Research. *America's Continuing Revolution: Eighteen Distinguished Americans Discuss Our Revolutionary Heritage.* Garden City, N.J.: Doubleday Anchor Books, 1976.

Avins, Alfred, ed. *The Reconstruction Amendments' Debates: The Legislative History & Contemporary Debates in Congress on the 13th, 14th & 15th Amendments.* Richmond: Virginia Commission on Constitutional Government, 1967.

Bailyn, Bernard. *The Ideological Origins of the American Revolution.* Cambridge, Mass.: Harvard University Press, 1967.

Bauer, Elizabeth Kelley. *Commentaries on the Constitution.* New York: Columbia University Press, 1952.

Carey, George W. *In Defense of the Constitution*. Indianapolis: Liberty Press, 1995.

Corwin, Edward. *The "Higher Law" Background of American Constitutional Law*. Ithaca: Cornell University Press, 1965.

———. Edward S. Corwin's *The Constitution and What it Means Today*. 14th ed., revised by Harold W. Chase and Craig R. Ducat. Princeton: Princeton University Press, 1978.

The Federalist Concordance, edited by Thomas S. Engeman, Edward J. Erler, and Thomas B. Hofeller. Chicago: The University of Chicago Press, 1988.

Franck, Matthew J. *Against the Imperial Judiciary: The Supreme Court vs. the Sovereignty of the People*. Lawrence: The University of Kansas Press, 1996.

Franklin, John Hope. *Reconstruction: After the Civil War*. Chicago: The University of Chicago Press, 1961.

Friedrich, Carl J., and Robert C. McCloskey. "The Roots of American Constitutionalism." Introduction to *From the Declaration of Independence to the Constitution*. New York: Liberal Arts Press, 1954.

Frisch, Morton, and Richard Stevens, eds. *American Political Thought: The Philosophic Dimensions of American Statesmanship*. New York: Charles Scribner's Sons, 1971.

Goldwin, Robert A., and Robert A. Licht, eds. *The Spirit of the Constitution: Five Conversations*. Washington, D.C.: The AEI Press, 1990.

Griffin, Stephen M. *American Constitutionalism: From Theory to Politics*. Princeton: Princeton University Press, 1996.

Hamilton, Alexander, James Madison, and John Jay. *The Federalist Papers*. New York: Mentor Books, 1961.

Horwitz, Robert H., ed. *The Moral Foundations of the American Republic*. 3d ed. Charlottesville: University Press of Virginia, 1986.

Hyneman, Charles S., and Donald S. Lutz, eds. *American Political Writing during the Founding Era*. 2 volumes. Indianapolis: Liberty Press, 1983.

Hyneman, Charles S. *The Supreme Court on Trial*. New York: Atherton Press, 1963.

Jaffa, Harry V. *How to Think About the American Revolution: A Bicentennial Cerebration*. Durham, N.C.: Carolina Academic Press, 1978.

Jaffa, Harry V. *Original Intent & the Framers of the Constitution: A Disputed Question.* Washington, D.C.: Regnery Gateway, 1994.

———. *The Crisis of the House Divided: An Interpretation of the Issues in the Lincoln-Douglas Debates.* Garden City, N.Y.: Doubleday & Company, 1959.

Jefferson, Thomas. *Jefferson's Writings.* Edited by M. Peterson. New York: The Library of America, 1984.

Kent, James. *Commentaries on American Law.* Boston: Little, Brown, and Company, 1884.

Kurland, Philip B., and Ralph Lerner, eds. *The Founders' Constitution.* 5 volumes. Chicago: University of Chicago Press, 1986.

Lincoln, Abraham. *Abraham Lincoln: Speeches and Writings.* 2 volumes. Edited by Don E. Fehrenbacher. New York: The Library of America, 1989.

McDonald, Forest. *Novus Ordo Seclorum: The Intellectual Origins of the Constitution.* Lawrence: The University of Kansas Press, 1985.

McDowell, Gary L. *Equity and the Constitution.* Chicago: The University of Chicago Press, 1982.

McIlwain, Charles H. *The American Revolution: A Constitutional Interpretation.* New York: Macmillan, 1924.

McLaughlin, Andrew C. *The Confederation and the Constitution, 1783-1789.* New York: Crowell-Collier, 1962.

Mansfield, Harvey C., Jr. *America's Constitutional Soul.* Chicago: The University of Chicago Press, 1981.

Morgan, Edmund S. *The Birth of the Republic.* Chicago: The University of Chicago Press, 1977.

Pangle, Thomas L. *The Spirit of Modern Republicanism: The Moral Vision of the American Founders and the Philosophy of Locke.* Chicago and London: The University of Chicago Press, 1988.

Rossum, Ralph A., and Gary L. McDowell, eds. *The American Founding: Politics, Statesmanship, and the Constitution.* Port Washington, N.Y.: Kennikat Press, 1981.

Stevens, Richard G. *The American Constitution and its Provenance.* Lanham, Md.: Rowman & Littlefield, 1997.

Storing, Herbert J. *What the Anti-Federalists Were For.* Chicago: The University of Chicago Press, 1981.

Story, Joseph. *Commentaries on the Constitution of the United States*. 3 volumes. New York: Da Capo Press, 1970.

Thurow, Sarah Baumgartner, ed. *Constitutionalism in America*. 3 volumes. I. *To Secure the Blessings of Liberty: First Principles of the Constitution*. II. *E Pluribus Unum: Constitutional Principles and the Institutions of Government*. III. *Constitutionalism in Perspective: The United States Constitution in Twentieth-Century Politics*. Lanham, N.Y., London: University Press of America, 1988.

Wolfe, Christopher. *The Rise of Modern Judicial Review*. Lanham, Md.: Littlefield Adams, 1994.

Wood, Gordon S. *The Creation of the American Republic. 1776–1787*. New York: Norton, 1972.